# START AND RUN A
# DESKTOP PUBLISHING BUSINESS

# START AND RUN A
# DESKTOP PUBLISHING BUSINESS

Barbara A. Fanson

**Self-Counsel Press**
*(a division of)*
International Self-Counsel Press Ltd.

USA           Canada

*Self-Counsel Press acknowledges the financial support of the Government of Canada through the Book Publishing Industry Development Program (BPIDP) for our publishing activities.*

*Printed in Canada.*

*First edition: 1997; Reprinted: 1998*

*Second edition: 2004*

**National Library of Canada Cataloguing in Publication**

Fanson, Barbara A., 1959-
  Start and run a desktop publishing business/Barbara A. Fanson.—2nd ed.


  (Self-Counsel Press business series)
  First ed. published under title: Start and run a profitable desktop publishing business.

  ISBN 1-55180-428-X

  1. Desktop publishing industry—Management. 2. New business enterprises. I. Fanson, Barbara A., 1959- . Start and run a profitable desktop publishing business. II. Title. III. Series: Self-counsel business series.
    Z286.D47F36 2003  686.2'2544536'06  C2003-906203-5

**Self-Counsel Press**
*(a division of)*
International Self-Counsel Press Ltd.

| | |
|---|---|
| 1704 N. State Street | 1481 Charlotte Road |
| Bellingham, WA 98225 | North Vancouver, BC V7J 1H1 |
| USA | Canada |

*To my friend and mentor Nina Coco who always encourages me to do my best.*

*Nina encourgages entrepreneurship. One time she said that if I could invent self-cleaning windows, she'd take ten orders.*

*Personally, I think self-paying bills would be more beneficial.*

# *CONTENTS*

# INTRODUCTION

For some, desktop publishing was a natural evolution from the traditional graphic arts industry of typesetting and paste-up. To some, learning how to do desktop publishing became a necessity. And to others, desktop publishing seemed like an exciting career change.

This book is written for publishers, designers, writers, marketing specialists, Web page designers, photographers, video editors, and presentation experts who have grown into the desktop publishing industry, and now have a burning desire to strike out on their own. It is also written for those who, because of economic conditions, cannot find full-time employment and are forced to work by contract.

If you are planning to start a freelance business in a related field such as writing, editing, designing, Web page design, photography, marketing, or multimedia, this book will provide insight into these related vocations.

This book offers advice on how to start your business — from registering a business name, to producing artwork efficiently, to invoicing and collecting your fees. Whether you are just starting out or have been operating a business for years, you will gain valuable information on how to become more profitable and more efficient.

Operating your own business requires self-motivation, perseverance, and a talent for time management. Operating a desktop publishing business will also require a good sense of design, computer software knowledge, and an understanding of the printing industry. If you enjoy challenges and performing different functions daily, a desktop publishing business may be the answer for you.

Desktop publishing forces individuals to become super designers. As technological advances make it easier to produce artwork and make changes, a desktop publisher must know how to measure and recognize typefaces, typeset properly, develop good design skills, operate a scanner, proofread, and increase his or her understanding of trapping, stripping, and printing, as well as market the business and deal with clients. It is difficult to find all of these talents in one person.

And it is easier still to make mistakes. Traditionally, graphic artists were specialists in one segment of the production process. They were typesetters, markup specialists, paste-up artists, proof-readers, or film strippers. Today, we expect one person to be able to perform all of these functions — and to do them all well.

If you are planning to start your own desktop publishing business, ask yourself some questions: Why do you want to start a business? Do you believe it can be profitable? Are you prepared to make sacrifices in order to succeed? Do you have the talent and knowledge to produce good quality artwork?

The desktop publishing industry has changed dramatically in the last 15 years. In the early 1990s, there were very few people with computers and the high-end graphic software necessary to produce publications and promotions, so freelance work was easy to find. Most desktop publishing was done on a Macintosh computer since most of the graphic software such as Adobe Photoshop and QuarkXPress were only available on a Macintosh computer. By the mid-1990s, these graphic software programs became available on a Windows computer so more people had access to the software. By the year 2000, a lot of publications and promotions were being done on a Windows computer, though Macintosh has remained the favorite among graphic designers and advertising agencies.

The desktop publishing industry has also become much more competitive and freelance work is harder to find. With more affordable computers and software, more publications and promotions are being done within a company, so the need for free-lancers has dropped significantly. Administrative clerks, editors, photographers, marketing specialists, and Web page designers have bought and learned the software and are now producing artwork that would have been done by desktop publishers. Much of the work that would have been contracted out to a freelancer is being done internally. So where do desktop publishers find work in the competitive desktop publishing industry? Read on.

## CHAPTER *1*
# WHAT IS A DESKTOP PUBLISHER?

*No matter how great the author's wisdom or how vital the message or how remarkable the printer's skill, unread type is merely a lot of paper and little ink. The true economics of printing must be measured by how much is read and understood and not by how much is produced.*

— HERBERT SPENCER

In 1984, Paul Brainerd, of Aldus Corporation, coined the phrase "desktop publishing" to describe the artwork that could be created using Aldus's page layout software program. Using a 300 dots per inch (dpi) laser printer hooked up to the computer, you could print out black-and-white, camera-ready artwork. A lot has changed since then. Today, you can take your file to a service bureau or commercial print shop to be output on paper, film, or color printout with up to 3,300 dpi. The quality has improved immensely.

*1*

A desktop publisher is a person who uses a computer to produce artwork that can be printed. Desktop publishing is the process of publishing artwork from the top of a desk. Personal computers can be used to produce publications, brochures, advertisements, business forms, sales literature, coupons, flyers, and much more. Desktop publishers should be prepared to design, typeset, and produce a variety of publications and sales literature, including:

**Publications**

- Magazines
- Newsletters
- Newspapers
- Bulletins
- Journals

**Sales literature and promotional materials**

- Brochures
- Booklets
- Flyers
- Coupons
- Direct mail materials

**Business forms**

- Invoices
- Contracts/agreements
- Purchase orders
- Project dockets
- Time sheets

**Business stationery**

- Letterhead
- Envelopes
- Business cards
- Mailing labels

**Instructional materials**

- Course manuals
- Course handouts
- Overhead transparencies

- Certificates
- Display cards

As well, desktop publishers may be asked to produce other materials which are not really desktop publishing but may be produced by a computer. These include:

- Signage (interior and exterior)
- Point-of-purchase materials
- Packaging
- Electronic presentations
- Web page design
- Multimedia presentations
- Video editing
- Animation

Desktop publishing. Anyone can do it. But how many people can meet promised deadlines, satisfy the client, and make money?

Specialize in an area that cannot be performed by internal staff.

## Who Needs Desktop Publishing?

Ten years ago, organizations hired outside vendors for three reasons:

(a) To implement ideas that were conceived internally, such as mechanical art. But today, inexpensive computers and easy-to-use software allow companies to do much of the production internally. For example, corporate newsletter editors used to write the stories and hire companies to typeset and paste-up the newsletter. Today, editors are writing and producing the entire newsletter on a computer.

(b) To handle overflow work and temporary projects. However, projects can now be completed much faster because of computers, so there isn't as much overflow work available. There are more freelancers, so overflow work is harder to get, lower paying, and more demanding.

(c) To create projects that require special expertise, such as corporate identity, color publications, package design, illustrations, presentations, multimedia, or speech writing. Today, talent, skills, and expertise may not exist in organizations. The amount of high-level work that is farmed out has increased. Organizations may not have enough internal staff to handle important assignments such as signage, trade show exhibits, corporate marketing plans, or press releases, so they'll hire freelancers to fill this void.

Low-end creativity has virtually vanished, the middle segment (overflow work) is increasingly unproductive, but the high-end (special assignments) is flourishing. To have your own successful desktop publishing business, you need to specialize in an area that cannot be performed by internal staff. Develop a market niche for yourself. For example, a corporate newsletter editor could produce a black-and-white newsletter, but could he or she create color newsletters and publications? This is just one area you could specialize in. How you can develop a market niche is discussed in more detail in Chapter 2.

## The Self-Employed Desktop Publisher

The terms "freelancer" and "self-employed" refer to anyone who works for himself or herself, including independent contractors, small business owners, entrepreneurs, consultants, photographers, writers, designers, and desktop publishers. Successful self-employment is about discovering your uniqueness and spreading the word.

As a desktop publisher, you can perform your service in a variety of ways. As a *freelancer*, you may work in other people's offices and be paid hourly, daily, or per job. You might also choose to be a *temp*, working for a temporary personnel agency. When the agency calls to see if you're available for work, you can say yes or no.

You could have a *special deal* or arrangement with a printer, public relations firm, advertising agency, or market researcher. It could provide office space in exchange for services, or printing in exchange for desktop publishing.

With a *sharing agreement*, you could share an office or equipment with another desktop publisher or organization: one does sales while the other uses the equipment. This setup is similar to a time-sharing setup.

If you know a lot about a certain subject, you could promote yourself as a *trainer or consultant*, and turn your knowledge into money. Training and seminars have been very popular during the 1990s.

If you can do something unique, you're a *specialist* and can throw out all the rules and establish your own fee.

There are also lots of opportunities for desktop publishers who have a well-rounded knowledge of software and print production. Why not:

(a) Start your own business.

(b) Freelance for printers, advertising agencies, and in-house art departments.

(c) Work on a contract basis for printers, advertising agencies, and in-house art departments.

(d) Work for a temporary placement agency.

(e) Become a print broker obtaining assignments from various clients and sub-contracting the work to other desktop publishers.

## CHAPTER 2

# THE MARKET AND OPPORTUNITIES

*Too many men, to their detriment, ignore intuition and suffer from "Analysis Paralysis."*

— ROY ROWEN

Before registering your business and buying any equipment, it's important to analyze yourself and your business objectives to determine if desktop publishing is right for you. Do you have a combination of business savvy and design expertise?

## What Is Success?

What does success mean? Some people measure success in dollars or the material things that money can buy. For others, power, status, and being at the top of their particular field are very important. Some self-employed people just want to make ends meet — on their own terms.

Perhaps success is the ability to achieve the objectives you set for yourself. You will achieve your goals if they are based on your own hopes and beliefs, rather than on those of society, your family, or anyone else.

Here are four tips to achieving your objectives in the shortest length of time:

(a) Define success for yourself.

(b) Be specific about your goals.

(c) Write down what has to be done to achieve each of your goals.

(d) Establish deadlines for your goals.

Your long-range goals should be broken down into manageable steps that can be implemented on a daily or weekly basis.

According to the book *Working for Yourself: A Guide to Success for People Who Work Outside the 9 to 5 World*, by Phillip Namanworth and Gene Busnar, success is defined as "the process of achieving all the possibilities in one's work and personal life that one is capable of."

## Evaluate Yourself

What are your talents? What are your areas of weakness? Before starting any business, it's important that you analyze yourself to see if you're an entrepreneur. Worksheet 1 has some questions that you should ask yourself before going any further.

## The Marketing Plan: Developing a Market Niche

Develop a market niche that will be in demand today and tomorrow. Before starting your own business or altering an existing business, you must analyze your skills and the market. What are your strengths? Does your city or town need your skills? Would there be enough work to support you?

### Specialize

When creating your marketing plan, think about ways in which you can specialize. Specialize in an area that the average corporate staff member isn't adept at. Most staff members of companies other than perhaps the large corporations cannot produce multimedia presentations, edit video tapes, create color publications, brochures, or sales literature, or design fill-in business forms that can also be used as mailing lists.

## Worksheet 1
## Evaluate Yourself

1. Why do I want to start a business? _____
   _____

2. What services can I offer my clients?_____
   _____

3. Do I have a specialty or special skills?_____
   _____

4. Do I have experience working in any particular business areas, such as health care, high tech, industrial, retail? If yes, which areas? _____
   _____

5. How would I describe the quality of my work in the following areas on a scale of 1 to 5, with 5 being excellent? (Consider concentrating on the areas that rate 4 or 5. If any of the items in the right-hand column rate lower than 4, you should consider whether desktop publishing is really the right business for you.)

   _____Developing design concepts          _____Doing color separations

   _____Translating ideas in to designs     _____Doing illustrations

   _____Creating interesting, effective layouts  _____Copy writing

   _____Typography                          _____Editing

   _____Desktop publishing                  _____Production management

6. Do I have a particular design style? How would you describe your artwork: conservative, imaginative, sophisticated, etc.? _____
   _____

7. Which elements of my design style are most interesting?_____
   _____

8. How consistent is the level of quality of my work? If it varies, when does it vary, and why? _____

_____

9. Are there any elements that will date my look in a year? _____

_____

10. Do I change my styles or work often to what's trendy? Does that affect the way my work looks? _____

_____

11. What projects have I enjoyed most? Disliked most? _____

_____

12. Which of the following describe my attitude toward the work I want to do? (*Place a check mark next to any that apply, and then consider how you can develop your business to reflect both these words and needs.*)

   ❑ I prefer to stick with what I know well and do well.

   ❑ I like to do a variety of activities daily.

   ❑ I'm a go-anywhere, do-anything kind of person.

   ❑ I can stick with one job until it's done.

   ❑ I'd love to work with four-color all the time.

   ❑ I really enjoy the challenge of doing quality work on a limited budget.

   ❑ I prefer collaborating with, rather than working for, clients.

   ❑ I do my best work when I'm left alone to develop my ideas.

   ❑ I prefer working with clients who know what they want.

   ❑ I'd rather have the freedom to develop my own concepts on a project.

☐ Producing color separations is boring.

☐ I'd rather watch projects come together when I do the separations.

☐ I'd rather have a number of short-term projects I can finish quickly.

☐ I'd rather work on long-term projects, getting in at the beginning and developing them gradually over time.

13. How would I rate my performance in these areas on a scale of 1 to 5, with 5 being excellent? (*Again, if you rate any of these items lower than 4, you should consider whether desktop publishing is the right business for you.*)

___ I know how to position clients in their markets.

___ I can analyze clients' market and their competition.

___ I can give clients the best possible price.

___ I can help clients decide what's best for their projects.

___ I am good at keeping clients informed about their projects.

___ I can meet deadlines.

___ I can stay within a budget.

___ I can turn projects around quickly.

14. Who are my present clients? Which clients will continue to give me work? Where are they located? What kinds of businesses are they in? _____

_____

1 5. What kinds of projects will my clients give me? _____

_____

16. How easy or difficult do I find these projects to work with? Why? _____

_____

17. How profitable are the clients to me? _____

_____

18. How much money do I expect to make from my business?_____

_____

### Market to mid-sized companies

Promote yourself to mid-sized companies. Many large corporations have art departments capable of creating sales literature and publications. Small businesses, on the other hand, are sometimes difficult to deal with because they want everything for nothing, yesterday, and don't know how to explain what they want.

Market yourself to mid-sized companies that are too small to have an art department but large enough to pay their bills promptly. Mid-sized companies may need price lists, advertisements, flyers, catalogues, newsletters, sales literature, and business forms prepared for them.

Find an industrial area near your business and market your services to those businesses by telephone or direct mail.

### Target frequent publications

If you specialize in frequent publications, you will have the same clients monthly, bimonthly, or quarterly. After you create the first issue (newsletter, magazine, journal, or newspaper), you can copy the file to produce the next issue. You'll have to set up style sheets, master pages, headers and footers, paragraph formatting, and layout the publication only once.

It is fairly easy to market to publications. Everywhere you go, you'll find newsletters — at the library, at a trade show, even through the mail. Contact the editor whose name and telephone number is listed in the masthead; you can do a telephone sales call to get new business.

### Create your marketing plan

Create a marketing plan to help you focus on your goal and to make sure you're moving in the right direction. A marketing plan provides a road map for your business. When you know your destination, you'll know which road to take to reach it. Sometimes the road will have ruts, but if you review your marketing plan periodically, you can determine what will get you back on your path.

Use Worksheet 2 to analyze your business and establish a marketing plan.

The marketing plan should cover four main areas: product, place, price, and promotion.

(a) *Product:* The product portion of the marketing plan explores how you're going to specialize and what product

## Worksheet 2
## Developing a Marketing Plan

**Product:**

What product or service will you offer? _____

_____

What are your personal strengths? _____

_____

How is your business unique? _____

_____

Who is your competition? _____

What is your market? _____

Who are your potential clients? _____

_____

**Place:**

Where will you set up your office? _____

What furniture will you need? _____

_____

What equipment is necessary? Optional? _____

_____

What software is necessary? Optional? _____

_____

What stationery will you need printed? _____

What office supplies will you need? _____

_____

## Worksheet 2 — Continued

**Price:**

What is the average price in the industry for services you will provide? _____

_____

What are your overhead costs? _____

_____

What are your project expenses? _____

Will you charge by the hour, page, or product? _____

Will your price include project expenses such as diskettes, fax transmissions, couriers, and telephone calls? _____

What will you include in your agreement, contract, proposal, and estimate? _____

_____

Who owns the final art? _____


**Promotion:**

How will you promote yourself? _____

_____

How will you present yourself? _____

_____

Who is your potential client, and how can you reach him or her? _____

_____

What associations should you join? _____

How will networking help you get a client? _____

or service you're going to offer. How will your product or service be different — or better — than the competition?

(b) *Place:* Where will you operate your business? Can you set up an office in your home or will you need to rent office space? Chapter 6 discusses in more detail setting up your office and equipping it.

(c) *Price:* How much should you charge for your service? How does your price compare with the competition? Chapter 4 focuses on pricing your work.

(d) *Promotion:* What's the best method of reaching your potential client? What publications does your potential client read? There are several methods of promoting your business, as discussed in Chapter 8.

Because so many companies are downsizing, they have reduced specialized departments, including those that produce publications. It is cheaper for them to hire freelancers on an "as-needed" basis rather than employ a full-time staff member. The prolonged recession has brought about this positive niche.

## The Business Plan

A business plan is different from a marketing plan. The marketing plan focuses on product, place, price, and promotion. Who are your clients, what product will you sell them, how much will you charge them, and where do you find them? The business plan, on the other hand, deals with how the business will operate and its financial aspects.

The business plan is a list of proposed activities that will enable you to fulfill your business objectives. It is one of the most effective management tools a business can employ, and can be used to negotiate major trade credits with your suppliers and to support your goals.

A business plan is necessary for obtaining financial aid. As well, it allows you to test the validity of your idea and provides you with a game plan. A typical business plan consists of four main elements: introduction, business concept, financial plan, and appendix.

Your business plan should follow the basic format outlined below.

(a) Introductory page (one page)

Includes the business name, address, phone number, and a brief description of the business.

(b) Table of contents (one page)

Contents of your business plan listed by headlines, with page numbers.

(c) Summary (one–two pages)

Main body of your plan with key points on why you are starting the business and what you have to offer. You have five minutes to sell!

(d) Description of the industry (one page)

Documented information, new product data, and details of trends.

(e) Description of your venture (one page)

Unique aspects, description of developmental work you've done.

(f) The marketing plan (at least one page)

Take the marketing plan you have created, by answering the questions in Worksheet 2, and incorporate them into this part of the business plan. You should be answering these questions: How are you selling the product or service? How are you distributing it? At what price? What are your promotion plans? What guarantees do you offer? How will you present the product or service to the client?

(g) Corporate structure (one page)

Detail ownership, partners, and their résumés. Include an organizational chart, if necessary.

(h) Risk assessment (one page)

Assess hazards to start up, competition outlook, and financial risks. Detail your contingency plan if there is a crisis.

(i) The financial plan (at least one page)

Include sales forecast, cost estimates, pro forma statements (balance sheet), projected profit and loss statement, cash flow forecast (Worksheet 3), financing, capitalization.

(j) Appendix

Include letters from present clients, suppliers, letters of reference, documents including registration or letters of incorporation, pricing agreements, leases and agreements.

See *Preparing a Successful Business Plan*, another book in the Self-Counsel Series, for further details on creating a business plan.

## CHAPTER 3

# MAKING YOUR BUSINESS LEGAL

*The cost of doing business is nothing compared with the cost of not doing business.*

— *UNKNOWN*

## Naming Your Business

Your business needs a name if you want to be taken seriously. Linda Bell, a desktop publisher in Toronto, took a long time to decide on a name for her business. She had to be careful choosing a business name with "Bell" in it, because the local telephone company was called Bell Canada. Linda chose the name Bell Imaging because she works with images on the screen. Linda didn't want to use the words "desktop publishing" because she was afraid it would date the business.

A memorable business name will reinforce the image you wish to project. A name with flair will make it easier for people who hear about your business to remember you. I changed my company name to Sterling Communications in 1984 after a boyfriend started a new business called Regency Enterprises, named after his car. I thought "regency" sounded regal, so I called mine "sterling." I chose "communications" because it could be used in publishing, writing, and designing. Because "sterling" is a popular word, many people think they've heard of me before.

Avoid initials unless you're prepared to spend a lot on promoting what they mean. If you're a designer, you might start with an image or logo, then choose a name. The logo should be a reflection of your business. If your business card is conservative, is your style of artwork also conservative?

You should register the name of your business to protect that name by filing with county or provincial authorities. The name you have chosen will be checked against previously filed names to ensure that the name has not been taken by another business. This is for your protection, too. Once your name is on file, it cannot be used by anyone else in that district.

Many people start their businesses and do not register the name. This can be a costly mistake. You may operate for a few months or longer, all the while spending time and money to get your business's name recognized and respected, then one day you receive a registered letter in the mail telling you to stop using it. Too late, you find out that the name is already used and protected by someone else. You may even be liable for damages.

It is a good idea to have two, or even three, names ready before you register. That way, if your first choice is rejected, you have another name ready, and you don't have to start all over again. A quick — though not foolproof — way to check the availability of the name is to scan your local telephone book.

In Canada, you can have a name search done through the provincial ministry that handles incorporations. This will also tell you if the name is registered out of province. This process takes about a week and there is a small fee, generally under $50.

In the United States, your city or county clerk will tell you if the name you have chosen is available for use.

Don't order expensive stationery and business cards before "saving" your name: you could end up out of pocket. You can always use your whole personal name — Donna Silk, for example, and you do not have to register it. But if you are using only part of

A business can be formed as a sole proprietorship, a partnership, or a corporation.

your name — for instance, Donna's Desktop Publishing — you should register it. As well, if you carry on business with a name other than your own, or add anything to your name such as "& Associates" or "Designs," you must register the name.

## Business Registration

A business can be formed as a sole proprietorship, a partnership, or a corporation. You should choose the business structure most suitable for your business. Do you wish to function as a corporate or non-corporate entity? There are tax advantages and disadvantages in each of the business structures, and incorporation is governed by state or provincial laws. You should obtain legal and tax advice before making your final decision.

Registering your business does not include a name search. You are responsible for ensuring that the name is not already in use. Government addresses are listed in the appendix or you can check your telephone directory for a location near you.

### Sole proprietorship

Sole proprietorship is the most popular legal structure among freelancers, home-based businesses, and small businesses. It is the simplest and least expensive way to start out. Some businesses start this way and incorporate later. The sole proprietorship and the owner are one entity in the eyes of the government.

#### Advantages

- Low start-up costs
- You may have a lower rate of taxation
- Greatest freedom from regulation
- Owner in direct control
- Minimal working capital requirements
- Business losses can sometimes be used to offset other income (check with an accountant)
- All profits go to the owner

#### Disadvantages

- Unlimited liability: you are personally liable for all your business debts
- Lack of continuity

- Some government loans or guarantee programs are not available to the sole proprietor
- It can be difficult to raise capital

## Partnership

Partnerships must be registered with the appropriate government agency

### Advantages

- Low start-up costs
- Ease of information
- Additional sources of venture capital
- Broader management base
- Possible tax advantages
- Limited outside regulation

### Disadvantages

- Unlimited liability
- Lack of continuity
- Divided authority
- Difficulty in raising additional capital
- Hard to find suitable partners

## Incorporation

While the corporate form of legal structure will cost more initially, it may be the right structure for you, depending on the nature of your business. Usually an incorporation is for one state or province, but you can get a federal incorporation, if you plan to operate or have branch operations in another state or province.

### Advantages

- Limited liability: you are not responsible for the corporation's debts
- Ownership is transferable
- Continuous existence
- Legal entity
- Possible tax advantages
- Easier to raise capital

- Easier to sell
- May be perceived by clients as having more status

*Disadvantages*
- Closely regulated
- Most expensive form to organize
- Charter restrictions
- Extensive record keeping necessary
- Double taxation

## Sales Tax Permits

You may require a sales tax number if your business buys goods for resale or purchases materials used in manufacturing a product — even artwork. This regulation may apply in all states and provinces that have a sales tax.

If you register and get a sales tax number, you will be collecting tax from the buyer of your product, and that tax must be remitted to the tax office.

In the United States, contact your state tax office, describe the nature of your business, and ask for the appropriate permit.

In Canada, contact the provincial tax department to obtain a provincial tax number.

**Note:** The goods and services tax (GST) was introduced January 1, 1991 in Canada and is applied to most goods and services produced there. Any business in Canada that supplies a product or service and grosses over $30,000 yearly must register and collect GST. Currently, it is 7 percent of the gross amount on an invoice. Medical firms, government agencies, foreign clients, and a few others are exempt from paying GST.

Your local Revenue Canada office will provide details on the tax and the filing requirements. Check the blue pages of your phone book. (At the time of writing, the Atlantic provinces had merged their provincial sales tax with the GST into the "harmonized sales tax," or HST. Contact your local tax offices for the latest details.)

If you register for GST you can claim all the GST paid on supplies purchased, so it may be beneficial to register for GST even if you aren't grossing $30,000 yearly. However, keeping track of GST does require extra bookkeeping.

## Zoning By-Laws

Before renting an office or setting up a home office, you might want to check with your local municipal or county office to find out if your location is zoned for commercial use. Are you legally allowed to operate a home-based business from your home?

Operating a business from home in a residentially zoned area has a few restraints. The restrictions are designed to protect neighborhoods from odor, noise, excess traffic, and pollution from businesses. Some of the restrictions may include not being allowed to sell retail, employ anyone other than family members, or store inventory.

If you rent an apartment or house, your landlord or apartment owner may have specific clauses in the rental and lease agreements prohibiting the use of rented space for business purposes. Now might be a good time to re-read your agreement.

## Business Insurance

Discuss your business and home insurance with a professional. A standard homeowner policy will not cover lawsuits, damages, or accidents that may result from your business.

Make sure you have adequate protection for your business and your home. If you start a business in your home without the proper insurance, you take the chance that it will void your existing coverage.

Some insurance companies will let you add a rider to your existing insurance to cover office furniture and business equipment such as computers, copiers, fax machines, etc.

When I used to work out of my home and had just one computer, I paid an insurance premium of about $500 annually. This covered the computer and office equipment and included liability, should someone have slipped and sued me.

## Start-up Information

While in the planning stage of starting a business, you should take advantage of the many sources of information available. Your bank or accountant may have booklets on preparing a business plan or the legal structure of your business.

## In the United States

In the United States, the Small Business Administration (SBA) offers a wide variety of publications covering topics such as budgets, market research, legal structure, marketing, and financing. To find out what's available, write to:

US Small Business Administration
P.O. Box 30
Denver, Colorado 20415

You can also call the SBA's Small Business Answer Desk toll-free at 1-800-368-5855 from Monday to Friday, 8:30 a.m. to 5:00 p.m. EST or visit the SBA Web site at <*www.sbaonline.sba.gov*> for an overview of what SBA offers.

SCORE, the Service Corps of Retired Executives, is a division of the SBA. If you need counseling of a specific nature, you may find a volunteer through SCORE who has experience in your business.

## In Canada

The main source of business information in Canada is the provincial government. Small Business Development is a department that can give you information on start-up help as well as federal programs that may prove beneficial.

The Business Development Bank of Canada (BDC) conducts seminars in a variety of business topics for a minimal fee. The BDC also has books and pamphlets to add to your reference material. If you do not have a BDC office near you, call its toll-free number: 1-888-INFO-BDC. You can access its extensive Web page at <*www.bdc.ca*> for more complete data.

The BDC also offers CASE (Counselling Assistance for Small Enterprise), a nationwide pool of experienced, mostly retired, businesspeople who work on a fee basis to assist small business. The charge for this service is nominal. CASE counselors can advise and assist with marketing strategies, business plans, and financial monitoring systems. They will also advise on advertising and promotion.

## CHAPTER 4
# RAISING THE MONEY

*Definition of business the art of transferring money from other people's pockets to mine.*

— *UNKNOWN*

Starting and running any business takes money. Without sufficient capital, a business can quickly become stressful and tiresome. If there's no money in the bank account to meet your monthly operating costs, your enthusiasm and motivation may suffer.

The cash required to start your business can come from a variety of sources: your personal savings, relatives and friends, banks, private investors, or the government. Most business funding comes from a combination of two or more of the above.

Desktop publishers, Web page designers, or anyone else relying on a computer to make money must remember to save money for a new computer every three or four years. Although you may increase the RAM (Random Access Memory) or hard disk memory during that time, eventually you will outgrow your old computer and want a faster computer with more features. So if you're planning on getting a bank loan to finance computer equipment, try to pay it off within three years so you're not still paying for an old computer when you want a new one. The more you use a computer, the faster and more efficient you will become and you'll need a computer that can keep up with your progress.

Graphic software programs are updated every 12 to 18 months so you may want to keep updating your software. How will you pay for it? Your initial software purchase will be between $3,000 and $5,000. Yearly upgrades will probably be about $1,500. Keep this in mind when you are budgeting your annual expenses.

## Personal Savings

If you have enough savings to run your business until it makes a profit, you'll be in the best position. You'll have no anxious lenders to account to and no financial responsibilities other than to yourself and your business — and no bank interest to pay. There is no better way to start a new business than debt free.

## Relatives and Friends

"Love money" provided by relatives and friends usually takes the form of an interest-free loan. The money is lent on trust and no collateral is required.

If the money is repaid promptly, both parties remain happy and satisfied. If not, the borrowed money can become a contentious issue that survives much longer than the business. There is a danger in mixing money with a personal relationship.

If you do start your business with love money, plan to repay the loan quickly out of the profits of the business. Make sure you have a backup payment plan should the business be unable to repay the debt.

To protect yourself and the lender, prepare a promissory note that outlines all the terms and conditions. A friend of mine lent another friend $3,000; the friend died of a stroke before the loan was repaid. There was no formal record of the loan.

## Banks

Surveys show that 80 percent to 90 percent of businesses use the bank as their main resource for borrowing money. Sometimes, home-based businesses have more difficulty receiving funding because they're not always taken seriously. Another reason is poor presentation. A banker must qualify you and your business as credit worthy. The banker needs accurate information demonstrating your commitment and expertise in operating the business. Make sure you have prepared a business plan outlining exactly what your business will do, how much it will charge, and how much money is required.

If you approach your bank about a loan to start your business or to buy equipment, the banker may ask for a cash forecast to determine whether the amount you're asking for is enough. See Chapter 5 for a discussion of preparing a six-month budget.

## Personal Financing Options

Rather than apply for a loan in the business' name, some entrepreneurs have taken out personal loans in their own names. While they still needed sufficient collateral to cover the loan, they did not have to advise the banker on all details of their business venture. Later, when the business began to grow and was able to pay off the debt, they switched to commercial borrowing. Usually this type of loan is called term financing: money received in a lump sum with a specified pay-back period that includes payment on the amount borrowed plus interest.

Obtaining a personal loan is sometimes the easiest method, especially when only a small amount of money is needed. A personal loan does not require a business plan and sometimes, the cost of the money can be less. As long as you have the collateral and can satisfy the bank of your ability to pay, you should have no difficulty obtaining this type of loan. This loan — principal and interest — will go into your business records as a loan from you. You borrow from the bank and your business borrows from you.

Some entrepreneurs have even used the line of credit available on their credit cards. Credit cards offer a quick alternative to bank financing if the amount required is small. Use caution if you use credit card financing to start your business. This money is expensive since the interest rate is high.

Before granting a personal line of credit or loan, your banker may ask you to provide a statement of personal worth — a snapshot of your financial health. You need to list what you own (assets) and what you owe (liabilities). The difference between the two determines your financial worth.

Obtaining a personal loan is sometimes the easiest method of financing.

## Private Investors

A private investor is hard to find. Some people looking for a private investor will run a classified ad in a local newspaper. This approach is very risky. Going into business with someone you know can be difficult; going into business with someone you don't know can be impossible. An investor who is willing to invest money with a stranger usually asks for several conditions, including control of the company or an extremely high interest rate.

Your accountant is a better source for finding private investors. The accountant may know someone willing to invest in a small business. Investors are usually cautious and will expect to see a business plan with complete and accurate information, as a bank would.

## Government

The governments of both the United States and Canada provide financial assistance to small business.

In the United States, the funding is administered through the Small Business Administration. The SBA's role is to help small business with education and finances.

In Canada, there are several federal and provincial government departments set up to provide financial and counseling services. The best source for information is the small business development department of your provincial government. Also check with the Business Development Bank of Canada, a Crown corporation which provides specialized funding to business projects.

Government lending is usually done as a last resort. Usually the government, in both the United States and Canada, offer loan guarantees rather than direct loans. Before approaching any government lending department for funds, make sure you're well prepared with a business plan.

Some government programs give loans or guarantee loans for incorporated businesses only.

## CHAPTER 5
# PRICING YOUR WORK

*Money is the sixth sense, without which you cannot enjoy the other five.*

— SOMERSET MAUGHAM

How much should you charge for your service? How much should you mark up outside expenses and resell to the client? The objective of any business is to provide an excellent service or product, cover your expenses, pay yourself, update software and equipment, and produce a profit.

## How Much Does It Cost to Do Business?

You should charge at least enough to cover the cost of doing business. The cost of doing business is based on your operating costs or overhead. To determine your operating costs, make a list of monthly expenses. This will likely include: rent; utilities; leasing equipment such as fax machine, computer, or photocopier; telephone; materials and supplies; insurance; advertising; taxes; payroll or personal draw (what you pay yourself); travel and

It takes more time and money to find a new client than to keep an existing one.

entertainment; memberships; publication subscriptions; trade show fees; petty cash; and postage. Some costs, such as taxes, occur on a yearly basis, so divide these by 12 to determine a monthly rate.

Worksheet 3 lists expenses you should consider when calculating your operating costs.

To calculate operating costs accurately, you should add start-up costs so they can be recouped over the next year. Maybe you're planning to spend $2,000 to start your business by purchasing business cards, stationery, self-promotional items, a telephone, equipment, furnishings, answering machine, or desk.

Using Worksheet 3 and the figures you use to calculate your operating costs, prepare a six-month budget to get an idea of how much money you will need to cover expenses for six months.

## A Formula for Determining Your Fees

Here's a pricing formula based on a desktop publisher just starting out with an office at home who also wants a salary of $2,000 a month to cover living expenses. Here are her monthly overhead costs:

| | |
|---|---|
| Home office rent ($\frac{1}{3}$ of home) | $250 |
| Utilities (including telephone) | 225 |
| Taxes | 500 |
| Insurance on equipment ($\frac{1}{12}$ of annual fee) | 50 |
| Car insurance ($\frac{1}{2}$ of car) | 60 |
| Equipment leases | 400 |
| Stationary and supplies (not project related) | 50 |
| Petty cash and postage | 50 |
| Travel (gas for car) | 80 |
| Salary | $2,000 |
| **TOTAL MONTHLY OPERATING COST** | **$3,665** |

Formula:

(a) Multiply the monthly operating cost by 12 to calculate yearly operating costs.

$3,665 x 12 = $43,980

## Worksheet 3
## Six-Month Budget

| | MONTH 1 | MONTH 2 | MONTH 3 | MONTH 4 | MONTH 5 | MONTH 6 |
|---|---|---|---|---|---|---|
| Opening cash balance | | | | | | |
| **CASH RECEIPTS:** | | | | | | |
| Cash sales | | | | | | |
| Accounts received | | | | | | |
| Other cash receipts | | | | | | |
| **TOTAL CASH RECEIVED** | | | | | | |
| **CASH DISBURSEMENTS:** | | | | | | |
| Furniture | | | | | | |
| Computers/software | | | | | | |
| Accounting/legal fees | | | | | | |
| Advertising | | | | | | |
| Travel expenses | | | | | | |
| Taxes, fees, licenses | | | | | | |
| Property tax | | | | | | |
| Salaries/wages | | | | | | |
| Employee benefits | | | | | | |
| Rent | | | | | | |
| Insurance | | | | | | |
| Interest/bank charges | | | | | | |
| Payment on loans | | | | | | |
| Maintenance/repairs | | | | | | |
| Courier charges | | | | | | |
| Telephone/fax | | | | | | |
| Utilities | | | | | | |
| Expenses/postage | | | | | | |
| Computer supplies | | | | | | |
| Miscellaneous | | | | | | |
| **TOTAL CASH PAID OUT** | | | | | | |
| **RECEIPTS LESS PAID OUT** | | | | | | |
| **CLOSING CASH BALANCE** | | | | | | |

The closing cash balance becomes the opening cash balance for the next month.

(b) Add the start-up cost to the yearly operating cost to determine yearly costs.

$2,000 + $43,980 = $45,980

(c) Divide the yearly cost by 48 work weeks in a year to calculate weekly costs.

$45,980 ÷ 48 = $957.92

(d) Divide the weekly total by 5 to get the daily cost. (You should aim to have 25 billable hours per week.)

$957.92 ÷ 5 = $191.58

(e) Divide the daily cost by 5, the average number of billable hours in an eight-hour day.

$191.58 ÷ 5 = $38.32

$38.32 is the minimum amount you can charge per hour in your first year of business if you want to cover your start-up costs, operating costs, pay yourself, and stay in business. This rate is based on working 48 weeks a year, so you can have four weeks of holidays or recover from an illness.

This rate calculates just a base rate; it does not take into consideration profit — more revenue than expenses. To make a profit, you should increase your hourly rate by at least $10 or $15 per hour.

Also consider when setting a base hourly rate the computer on which your business does desktop publishing. Computers and software need to be updated periodically, so you'll need to make — and save — extra money.

The average hourly fee for most beginning self-employed designers is $50 per hour.

## Matching Your Previous Wage

If you were making $30,000 a year at your last job, you'll want to make at least that now. With a little calculation, you were making about $15 per hour in an eight-hour day. Add the cost of paying for your own drug and dental benefits and taxes, and you'll want to make $20 or $25 an hour, if you're doing eight billable hours per day. But if you're like most sole proprietors, you can work only about five billable hours, with three unbillable hours a day. To operate the desktop publishing business by yourself with five billable hours daily, you'll need to charge at least $30 per hour.

That's one way of pricing your work, but not the most realistic one since this is not a question of how much you should charge, but rather a question of how much your business should charge. Your business has to pay for its operation, which includes your salary, and make a little extra to cover periods of drought — when the client's on vacation and doesn't have a job for you, for example.

Be prepared to tell the client how many hours it will take you to complete the project.

## Seven Ways to Charge

You can charge for your service in seven ways.

### Per hour

Charging your client by the hour for work performed is the most popular method of calculating a fee. To determine an hourly rate, calculate how much money is required monthly to cover your operating expenses plus make a profit. Divide this monthly total by 20, since there are about 20 business days in a month. This will give you the daily amount of revenue you need to make. Divide the daily amount by four hours per day to calculate how much you need to make per billable hour. For example, if you want to make $200 per day to meet expenses and make a profit, you'll need to charge at least $50 per hour.

You should also do a survey of other desktop publishers in your community. I did a small survey of Toronto desktop publishers and discovered the average hourly rate was $50 per hour. Some moonlighters were giving artwork away for $20 per hour, whereas studios with rented office space charged $100 per hour. The average markup on outside supplies ranged from 10 percent to 20 percent.

Be prepared to tell the client how many hours it will take you to complete the project.

### Per page

Once you decide how much you want to make an hour, you can calculate how much to charge on a per-page basis. For example, calculate how long it will take you to typeset and lay out a page in a newsletter. At first, it may take an hour to typeset and lay out a newsletter page. If you charge $60 per hour, you would charge $60 per page. As your speed and efficiency increase, you may be able to produce a page in 20 minutes, but still charge $60 per page.

### Per day

Desktop publishers may prefer a per-day rate based on how much they need to make per day to pay operating expenses and make a living. Consultants working in another company's office or someone filling a contract position, perhaps replacing someone on holiday or maternity leave, usually charge a per-day rate. A trainer could also charge a per-day rate for training on-site. When I provided computer training to staff at a police station daily for four months, I charged a per-day rate and invoiced every two weeks.

A per-day rate may be different than simply your hourly rate multiplied by the number of hours you will be working. If you will be working in a company's office and using its equipment, you might not charge as much as a desktop publisher who is using his or her own equipment and has an office to maintain. But remember, as a freelancer, you want to make more than the company's regular employee, since you won't be receiving medical benefits from the company. You will want to charge at least $20 per hour, or $140 per day if you are working seven hours per day. Or, you might negotiate a better rate if you have a contract for a certain number of days. If you are supplying the computer equipment, you might add an additional rate per day or per month for the use of your equipment. I know desktop publishers who are charging an additional $200 to $700 per month for the use of their equipment.

### Per head

A per-head fee is often charged when training people or consulting, along with an hourly fee. For example you may charge $60 per hour for private computer training. You might charge an additional $10 per hour per additional person attending the training. Or, you could charge $300 per person to teach a page layout program for 12 hours. Or, you might choose to charge $300 to teach a particular software program to someone, and charge half price for each additional person.

Determining a per-head rate is based on how much money you need to make to pay your operating expenses, pay yourself, and make a profit to pay for future computer upgrades and expansion.

### Per project

A per-project rate is a flat fee you charge for a particular project. This rate is based on how many hours you think it will take you to complete the project, multiplied by your hourly rate. Or, it could be a fee based on your past experiences.

If a client asks you for an estimate to produce a flyer and you reply with an hourly rate, the client will undoubtedly ask how many hours it will take you to produce the flyer. The client wants to know if it will cost $50 or $500. You may want to quote a flat fee for the project, rather than your hourly rate.

If you produce an advertisement or other desktop publication for a client on a regular basis, you will probably charge the same amount each time, though one might require more or less time than another. For example, if you charged $150 for producing the first advertisement, you might charge $150 per project for similar ads.

Occasionally, a client may give you a set project fee that was established by a previous desktop publisher. That client may expect you to match that rate.

## By flat rate

A flat fee might be arranged for once-only assignments, such as logo design. The fee for a logo design could vary from $150 to $10,000, depending on where the design will be used, how much the design will be used, how large the organization is that will be using the design, and how many people you have to present and persuade the client to accept the design.

You may charge a flat rate for a photograph, for scanning photos, or for an illustration. You may also charge a flat fee to produce informational graphics or typographic special effects.

## By retainer fee

Service consultants often charge a retainer fee per month for service support and usually make themselves available within 24 hours of a telephone call from a client. I charged a retainer fee once to an author who was publishing a book using a software program that she didn't know.

After designing a corporate identity, you may be on "standby" while the logo is applied to various company items. You may charge a retainer fee per month or per day to make yourself available while the logo is produced on these various materials.

Markup is a standard industry charge to cover administrative handling and processing of the account.

## Don't Start with a Low Fee

To determine a price for your service you could start by asking other desktop publishers how much they charge. But when self-employed designers say $50, $60, or $75 an hour, you may cringe at the fee. Since you're just starting out, you may think you're not worth that much. Maybe you've just learned the software program and you're not very fast yet. Whatever you do, don't start with a low hourly rate such as $20. You won't stay in business very long at that rate, and more importantly, it's difficult to increase your fee later. If it takes you twice as long to complete a project than other professional desktop publishers, then charge for only half the time.

## Variable Fee Scale

You might want to have a variable fee scale for different services you provide. For example, you might charge your highest hourly rate for concept development and design work, because this demands the most creativity, talent, and skill. Client consultations also require high-level communication skills and are arranged at the client's convenience, so you can also bill at a high rate. Paste-up and clerical work are often billed at a lower rate than creative work.

## Markup

Most desktop publishers add a markup, a standard percentage of the total, onto the cost of project materials and outside services. The average is 10 percent to 20 percent of the total. Some experienced designers add up to 35 percent of the total. Markup is a standard industry charge to cover administrative handling and processing of the account. It also covers all the extra paperwork and the use of your funds until the client re-imburses you, since you often have to pay the supplier before the client pays you.

Although it is all right to charge a markup, you shouldn't tell clients what the percentage is. Just quote the total cost including markup on estimates and invoices. If your printer charges you $500 for printing, you would add your markup, and invoice the client at the higher price.

## Budgeted Pricing

When you have a client who has a budget and is willing only to spend a certain amount, you may have to work your way backwards, allocating production costs, design and production time, overhead, and profit to match that amount.

For example, if the client has a budget of $1,000, deduct the production costs (imagesetting and printing), for example, $400. That leaves $600 for labor, overhead, and profit. Subtract $60, which is your 10 percent profit margin. The remaining $540 is the amount you can allow for labor and overhead costs. $540 divided by $40, for example (your hourly rate) equals 13.5. You can spend only 13.5 hours on the project to still make a profit.

Is 13.5 hours enough time to complete the project satisfactorily and meet the client's expectations? If you don't think you can do an outstanding job in 13.5 hours, you'll either have to lower your standards (which may not be wise), accept a lower profit, or decline the project.

## Working on Spec

Occasionally designers are asked to do work on speculation (on spec). That means you'll do the creative work, and if the client likes it, you might win the project. You're being asked to spend your time with no guarantee that you'll be paid for the work. You also have no guarantee that the client won't take your ideas and use them once you've been dismissed.

It's not unreasonable for a client to ask you to do a job on spec. Some clients think it's standard to see some sketches first. If you're just starting out and don't have any real work in your portfolio, you may have to work on spec to build your portfolio and your client base. But if you have a good portfolio that shows some well-executed projects, there is no reason why a client can't make a decision to hire you based on seeing your existing work.

If the client insists on seeing a few designs first, and you decide to take the job on spec "just this once," don't spend more than 10 percent of the time you estimate the entire job would take. Don't complete the brochure, for example.

Make sure the client understands up front that you're supplying only creative ideas or rough sketches, rather than a completed project. If this is not acceptable to the client, be prepared to walk away. When showing layouts to the client, make sure you put a copyright© symbol and the date on every piece you produce. Keep photocopies of all your work. This will help protect you if the client does intend to steal your designs.

When I was 20 years old and naive, I typeset and pasted-up a menu for a client. I supplied him with photocopies to proofread. When I came back to get the copies, he said he had decided not to use my work. A few weeks later I saw "my" menu on a printing press at my regular print shop. He was printing from the photocopies. Since I was a regular client of this print shop and the restaurant owner was not, my printer marked up the price of the printing and gave the extra to me.

Now, I fax proofs to clients with a copyright symbol printed on the page or I photocopy proofs onto off-white paper. I also stamp the page in a prominent location "Proof only. Not to be printed. Copyright [my name and the date]."

## Charges for Typical Projects

The following fee scale is what I charge for typical desktop publishing projects. Fees and rates will vary depending on who your client is (e.g., a large corporation or a non-profit society), the going rate in your location (e.g., the going rate in a large city may be drastically different from that in a rural area or smaller urban center), and your experience and operating costs, among other factors.

Printing, film output, and other outside supplies are not factored into these costs and should be considered as additional charges.

| | |
|---|---|
| 1-page flyer | $75 |
| 2-sided brochure | $200 |
| 4-page newsletter | $300 |
| 8-page newsletter | $500 |
| 16-page newsletter | $750 |
| 8-page tabloid newspaper | $1,120 |
| 40-page report | $1,000 |
| 1 typical Web page | $1,000 |

## CHAPTER *6*

# CHOOSING AND EQUIPPING YOUR OFFICE

*Good design does not have to shout. It can sit quietly on a page, barely noticed, yet it can be very effective.*

— BARBARA A. FANSON

To produce good quality artwork efficiently, you must have a clean, professional work environment with up-to-date equipment and organized storage space. Your office or studio could be located in a commercial print shop, typesetting or film house, advertising agency, in your home, or in a separate rented office.

## A Home Office

If you plan to work from home, you should have a separate room with a door that closes to keep family disruptions to a minimum. If you plan to claim a portion of household expenses as business deductions, you should have a separate room that is not used for anything else. For example, if you use one-third of your home for business, you may claim one-third of your rent or mortgage payment and other household expenses as a business expense. If later you are audited by the government, it could disallow this deduction if it finds you are using less than one-third of your home for business. (Years ago I used to work from home and claimed one third of the rent and utilities. When I was audited, no government agent ever came to my home; I simply mailed in the supporting documentation.)

If you plan to have a home-based business, your office space should ideally be at least 100 square feet or 10' x 10'.

## Advantages of a home office

There are several advantages to operating a business out of your home:

- Convenience; no commuting
- Reduced rental fees
- You can claim a portion of household expenses (insurance, utilities, property taxes, rent)
- Reduced start-up and operating costs
- Fewer financial restraints so you can grow
- Flexible work hours
- Minimal expenses for a second telephone line
- Reduced wardrobe expense
- Reduced daycare costs
- Family members can help out

## Disadvantages of a home office

There are a few disadvantages to operating a home-based business:

- Office may lack a professional appearance or atmosphere
- Family or friend interruptions
- Inability to separate work and home life
- Zoning by-laws and permits
- Space or storage limitations
- Lack of signage promotion
- Middle-of-the-night fax transmissions
- Napping, snacking, and home distractions
- Isolation or lack of companionship

- Difficult to hire employees
- Business activity could create difficulties with neighbors

## Renting Office Space

If you want a professional environment, or you outgrow a home office, or you've become so busy that you need to hire more staff, it's time to consider renting office space.

### Advantages of a rented office

- Space and storage can be negotiated
- Professional work environment for clients and employees
- Space may include boardroom facilities
- Walk-in clients can reduce travel expenses
- Signage or posters to promote your business

### Disadvantages of a rented office

- Expensive to rent
- Limits on natural lighting, renovations, furnishings
- May be inaccessible after hours
- Someone must be there at all times to greet unexpected visitors

## Rent a Mailbox

Operate your office out of a mailbox? Sure! A private mailbox service has many advantages that you can benefit from.

If you are out of the office frequently, how do you handle unexpected deliveries? A courier company will not leave a package without a signature. The answer? Use a private mailbox service.

Many mailbox services offer a choice of a P.O. Box number or a street address. Of course, the street address looks more professional. And you won't have to worry about zoning by-laws from your local government since the mailbox service is usually operated from a commercial location.

If you move, you won't have to print new business cards and stationery. Unfortunately, if you move to another city within Canada, Canada Post will not forward or re-address mail from a private mailbox to your new address.

A private mailbox service has many advantages that you can benefit from.

For a small monthly fee, you can have an address in a commercially-zoned area, a secure mailbox, responsible storage of received packages, a person always available to handle incoming packages, outgoing package pickup, shipping, copying, and a host of other services. Many private mailbox services also provide a fax transmission service for a per-page fee. A key may be supplied for after-hour entry.

## Furnishing an Office

Each business will have its own requirements for office furniture and equipment. If you plan to offer prepress or print production services, you may wish to purchase a drafting table and/or light table. To operate a desktop publishing business, you will require some furniture:

- Computer table with hutch for storage
- Printer stand
- Adjustable chair
- Storage shelves for filing books or disks
- Two-drawer filing cabinet which can be used as a counter top
- Desk with file drawers (optional)
- Drafting table/light table (optional)

## Equipping an Office

Some items will be necessary to equip an office, others optional. If you plan to do desktop publishing or multimedia, you'll need a fast computer with lots of RAM (random access memory) and hard drive storage. There are various types of computer systems you could set up.

The low-end system is suitable for home use, writers, and consultants, and includes a computer, monitor, CD-ROM (Compact Disc-Read Only Memory) drive, and laser printer. A color printer, scanner, modem, and external storage are optional.

The mid-range system is ideal for someone starting out as a desktop publisher and includes everything the low-end system has, as well as a scanner, modem, and external storage. A color printer is still optional.

The high-end system includes all of the above, as well as a color printer, which could be purchased later. If you're planning to provide multimedia services, you will require a video capture card and much more hard drive storage space.

Here is a partial list of computers and peripherals.

### Computer

Today, it doesn't really matter which computer platform you use — Macintosh or PC — most desktop publishing and multimedia software programs are made for either platform. The capabilities of the software and the operator are more important in desktop publishing than the brand of computer. QuarkXPress, Adobe Illustrator, Adobe Photoshop, and Adobe PageMaker are the most popular desktop publishing programs and are available in both computer platforms. Both platforms are virtually the same. CorelDRAW is a popular drawing program for Windows, and recently became available for Macintosh computers.

An estimated 90 percent of professional desktop publishers, graphic designers, prepress shops, and advertising agencies are using Macintosh computers. Journalists, corporate desktop publishers in large firms, and book publishers are using a mixture of Macintosh computers and PCs.

Before deciding on the computer platform best for you, ask family and friends what they use, ask your children what they're using in school, check magazine reviews, even attend a computer user group. Or take some computer classes on each platform to decide which one you prefer to work with.

Years ago, clients supplied text on IBM disks to be converted by a desktop publisher using a Macintosh computer. There are several software programs that make conversion much simpler today. If you purchase a Macintosh PowerPC, it comes with a Macintosh operating system, but you can add DOS to it. You can also put IBM-formatted disks into a Macintosh PowerPC and they won't beep. Page 69 outlines six ways of getting a story from WordPerfect on a PC to a designer who doesn't have WordPerfect on her Macintosh.

### Laser printer

After reading a story or document on the screen, you will want to output it so you can proof it more carefully. There are basically four kinds of printers for personal computers: dot matrix printers, ink jet printers, laser printers, and color printers. Your decision will be based on price and quality of output.

Desktop publishers do not use a dot matrix printer for outputting artwork. Instead, they use laser printers for outputting correspondence and business forms or a color inkjet printer for printing color proofs. Ideally, a desktop publisher should have both. A color inkjet printer is inexpensive to purchase, but the paper and ink cost more to replace than toner and paper for a black and white laser printer. A good black and white laser printer may require toner replacement a few times a year but it costs less than color ink.

If you plan to produce color separations from QuarkXPress or Adobe Illustrator, you will need a printer with a printer driver the software recognizes. Many desktop publishers output color separations to check their four-color work before taking it to a print shop for mass reproduction. If you're doing a four-color job, you should get four sheets of paper out of the printer; if you're not getting the required number of sheets, you can correct your file before proceeding to a print shop.

A black and white laser printer may have 600 or 1,200 dpi (dots per inch) and range from $600 to $2,500. A color laser printer ranges from $3,000 to $5,700. A color inkjet printer can be purchased from $100.

If your artwork just has type and rules, you could probably take your laser proofs to a commercial print shop for photocopying, if you're producing less than 1,000 copies. Most print shops can take your disk and output the file onto their laser printer or an imagesetter with more than 2,400 dpi. Some print shops can output film or printing plates directly from your computer file. Talk to your print shop before you start a project to discuss how to save the file, what software to use, and how to lay out the project.

### Scanner

Purchasing a desktop scanner for a computer will reduce halftone costs and production time.

You can scan logos, line art, black-and-white photos, color photos, or stories right into the computer. If a newsletter is output on a 1,270 dpi imagesetter at the service bureau, the art is camera-ready and in position — ready for the printing house. With a scanner, you don't need a film house or print shop to create halftones and photostats for you.

Images used in computer graphics programs must be in a digital pixel format. You can convert photographs to this format using specialized devices called scanners, digital still cameras, or video capture.

A scanner is similar to a photocopier: it bounces light off a document and converts the image to a series of very fine dots. Scanners intended for use with computers put these dots into a format that can be saved as a graphics file. With a graphics software program, you can import the file and edit the dots or copy the image.

Flatbed scanners and hand-held scanners allow you to scan artwork into the computer so you can add photos, logos, or illustrations to your publication or literature. Most serious desktop publishers avoid low-end, hand-held scanners because of their limitations. A flatbed scanner that sits on your desktop comes with scanning software to scan photos, logos, and illustrations into the computer. You can alter photos and illustrations with Adobe Photoshop or Corel PHOTO-PAINT!

You can also purchase OCR (optical character recognition) software to work with your scanner to scan text into the computer so it can be edited. This is a separate software program that scans each character into the computer so you can change the spelling, font, or style of the type.

### External storage device

Often desktop publishers will purchase an external storage device for transporting or archiving large files. This device hooks up to your computer and works like the hard drive built into your computer. You can install software or save electronic files on such a system.

External storage devices include Zip drives, Jaz drives, optical disk drives, or writable CD recorders. Most service bureaus have all these devices, in case you need to transport a large file. I've seen several files requiring over 30 megabytes of storage space to save them; that's about 23 high-density diskettes!

Compact disks (CDs) have also risen in popularity since most computers are now equipped with CD-ROMs. CDs are a method of archiving electronic files, storing photographs and images, and shipping software programs. Since CDs can hold up to 800 megabytes of information and only cost about $1 to duplicate, they are the choice of software manufacturers for shipping software. CDs are also more durable than other electronic storage methods. CD-ROMs can only read a file; you cannot save information on one, unless you purchase a writeable CD recorder, which are fairly inexpensive.

### Modem

With the popularity of the Internet, a modem has become a necessity for surfing the World Wide Web. You can use a modem, connected to a telephone line for slower, dial-up service, or you can

A modem transmits information from one computer to another through a telephone line.

get faster, high-speed service from a cable television company or telephone company, depending on the part of the country you live in. After paying a monthly fee to an Internet service provider, you could get Internet access, at least one e-mail address, and the space for uploading your own Web site.

## Digital Video Disk (DVD)

As of 2002, 20 percent of homes in North America have a DVD (Digital Video Disc) player connected to a television or a computer.

As a desktop publisher, you could create DVDs for your clients or to promote your own business. If you have a DVD-R (Digital Video Disc-Recordable), you can create DVDs from a blank DVD-R. If you purchase a DVD-R, it usually comes with basic software for creating slideshows from photos or video clips that were saved as QuickTime movies. You can also import QuickTime movies created with Macromedia Flash, though movie clips created within Flash will not work in a QuickTime movie.

A blank DVD-R costs more than a blank CD-R, but it holds more information. A blank DVD-R has come down in price to about $6 each. (I paid $55 for the first one I bought in 1998!) Each blank DVD-R holds about 4.6 gigabytes (GB). A CD-R can be purchased for about $1 and holds around 800 megabytes (MB).

A DVD-R is not like a CD that you just copy information to it and burn it. When you purchase a DVD-R, it usually comes with software for making a DVD. A DVD-R requires software for creating slideshows or playing video clips such as iDVD or DVD Studio Pro.

## Multimedia equipment

If you have a video camera and a computer with video capabilities, you can produce photos from video frame grabs. You can digitize videos or record computer work onto a video tape. You can also create self-running, interactive, electronic presentations for a client.

Some electronic presentation software such as Macromedia Director, Microsoft PowerPoint, and Macromedia Flash allow you to import video clips, music, photos, charts, and text into a presentation that can be viewed on a computer, projected onto a television screen, viewed on a Web page, or viewed from a CD or DVD.

It's possible to add video clips to a Web site; people can view the clips with high speed Internet service. If you have video-editing software such Adobe Premiere or Final Cut Pro, you can compress video clips for the Internet so their file sizes are smaller and take less memory.

Today's digital video camera can easily be hooked up to a computer by USB cable or IEEE (FireWire or I-Link) cable. Since the video is already in a digital form, it does not need to be converted from analogue to a digital signal with the help of a converter. You can plug the video equipment into a converter by S-VHS or composite cables (yellow, white, and red) and then the converter is plugged into a computer by USB or IEEE cable and the video and audio analogue files are converted to a digital file.

Some computers are loaded with basic video-editing software. Macintosh has iMovie and Windows has Movie Maker, which offer basic video editing capabilities such as sound effects, titles, clipping, and transitions between two different clips.

How much equipment required depends on what kind of presentation you plan to do. Here is some equipment to consider:

- *Computer with audio-visual (A/V)* capabilities. Some computers are equipped with A/V capabilities that allow you to capture and digitize video clips for use on a computer. With a digitizer, you can convert the analog signal from a television or video cassette recorder (VCR) to a digital signal for computer use. If you are thinking of editing videos, producing multimedia presentations, or creating Web page designs, consider getting a computer with built-in A/V capabilities.

- *Television.* You could hook up a computer to a consumer television, but there are less lines of resolution, so the quality would not be as good as your computer monitor. An industrial-style monitor or high-definition television is better.

- *Speakers.* Use to amplify the sound on your computer.

- *VCR* (video cassette recorder). Use to record presentations to be viewed with a VCR.

- *Video camera or camcorder.* Use to record your own video clips or freeze one of the 30 frames per second and use as a photo.

- *Sound mixer.* Use to maintain sound quality among several audio sources. For example, I found the sound recorded by my computer and camcorder were different when the video was played back. I have a Videonics Sound Effects Mixer for controlling sound quality. It also adds special effects and sounds.

- *Digital video mixer.* If you want to hook up several sources of video to your computer or video cassette recorder, consider a Videonics digital video mixer. It will take up to four sources, including a camcorder, VCR, and computer, and you can easily switch between them. You can also add a transition between two sources, so one source can fade or flip or slide into another.

- *Wireless lapel microphones.* Any good microphone will increase the sound quality of recorded voices. Consider a wireless lapel mike so you don't have to hold onto a microphone. The microphone can be plugged into a sound mixer or camcorder to record your voice.

### Digital camera

You'll save time and money with a digital camera. You can get photos in 29 seconds, and you don't require film, film processing, or scanning. You can snap photos and then download them onto a computer or you can take pictures while the digital camera is hooked up to the computer.

Some digital cameras take low-resolution images that are adequate for Web pages or e-mail messages, while other, more-expensive models have higher-resolution images for publications and promotions. As a desktop publisher, if you plan to purchase a digital camera, you should purchase a high-resolution model. Don't buy an inexpensive, low-resolution model just for the sake of owning a digital camera. Like other purchases, you should ask yourself what you plan to do with the camera and why do you need one?

Once you buy all the equipment and supplies, it costs nothing to take a photograph. Well, maybe. What will you do with your images once you take them? Your answer to this question will determine what type of camera you need and how many extras you'll have to buy, in addition to the digital camera. Purchasing a digital camera is not necessarily cheaper than a traditional camera, but the turnaround time is much faster.

#### Hidden Extras

Once you purchase a digital camera, you may need some additional equipment or supplies, depending on how you use your digital camera. If you're using the images on a Web page or computerized presentation, you won't require a printer. But, if you're planning to print your images, you may want a good ink jet printer, ink, and paper. And that's where the costs could add up.

A digital camera may require optional equipment:

- *Storage device for saving images:* If you keep downloading images from the camera's memory card to your computer, your computer's hard disk will eventually be filled and need to be emptied. You might want a CD burner to save your images on a compact disc (CD).

- *Color printer for outputting them:* Color inkjet printers have decreased in price greatly in the last ten years, but the real expense is the ink and specialized paper required for good output. You could also take your memory card or CD with images to a photo finisher for output. See your Yellow Pages for photo finishers that may offer output services.

- *Extra memory card:* The memory card that comes with the digital camera may hold a small quantity of images, so if you're planning to take a vacation or photograph a wedding, you will want more storage capability. Or, you could download your images to a portable computer or find a photo finisher that can burn a CD of your images.

- *Extra battery and battery charger:* If you're on vacation or photographing a wedding, the supplied battery for the digital camera may only be good for an hour, so a back-up battery is a worthwhile investment. Most digital cameras come with a battery charger.

- *Memory card reader to transfer images from the memory card to a computer:* Most digital cameras come with a cable to hook up the camera to a computer, but a memory card reader might be faster, more efficient or more convenient. I usually have my digital camera at home, but my computer and printer are at the office, so I just have to take the memory card to the office and insert it into the card reader, rather than taking the whole camera to the office.

- *Computer upgrades:* Your computer should be upgraded at least every four years so it can keep up with your progress.

- *Software for editing photos:* Many digital cameras come with Adobe Photoshop Elements, a basic, easy-to-use version of Adobe Photoshop.

- *Camera case for protecting the camera:* Some digital cameras do not come with a case, so you may have to pay extra to protect the camera.

### Advantages of a digital camera

There are a few advantages to owning a digital camera:

- You can take a hundred photos of your baby or pet and pick the one you want. Since it's hard to get a baby or pet to "hold that pose," you can take several photos and choose which ones to keep.

- If you don't like an image, delete it from the memory card or your computer after it's transferred to the computer. You don't have to print the images you don't like.

- Instant images. You don't have to wait for a photo finisher to develop the film and print the pictures.

- You can crop your photos or enlarge them if you have photo-editing software. Many digital cameras come with editing software.

### Disadvantages of a digital camera

There are a few disadvantages to owning a digital camera:

- Slow shutter speed means that an object that moves could be blurred in your photo. If you're taking a photo at a racetrack, the subject could have passed by the time your camera captures the image.

- Low-light conditions, such as inside a building, are difficult to photograph. Trying to take a photo at a wedding or a baptism in a church is probably the biggest challenge for a digital camera. Not only is the lighting in a church bad, but also there are often stained glass windows in the background. Your images from the digital camera may turn out dark.

- Small depth of field on digital cameras means that people about 10 feet away will probably be light enough, but anyone beyond that will be darker. The depth of field drops off greatly.

- How long will an inkjet-printed image last? No one knows for sure how long an image printed with an inkjet printer will last, but you can increase the length of time by storing them properly. Oxidants in the air are the worse culprits for fading your inkjet images, so place your printouts in a frame with glass or in a plastic sleeve. And keep your images out of direct sunlight. Better quality paper, inks, and special fixatif spray can also help maintain the quality and vividness of your printouts.

- Cameras with a higher resolution or more megapixels cost more. What will you do with your images taken with a digital camera? If your images will just be used on the Internet, a 3.1 megapixel camera will suit your needs. But if you are going to use your photos in a publication that will be printed on a printing press, you will need a higher resolution such as four or five megapixels or higher.

- Affordable models do not have changeable lenses. With a traditional 35mm camera, you could purchase a wide-angle lens, zoom lens, or filters, but with an affordable digital camera, you can't switch lenses.

The hidden extras could cost as much as the camera itself.

### Photo CD

Photo CD, developed by Kodak, is an exciting new imaging technology to store digital photographic images. Compact disks (CDs) offer optical disk technology for commercial applications including computer imaging, image archive and storage, image distribution, and image management. 35mm negative film and transparencies can be scanned to CD. Some new computers come with a built-in CD-ROM, or you can buy a CD-ROM as a peripheral for your computer. If you have a software program that allows you to import photographs, you can view your photographs on the computer.

When you take a roll of 35mm color film to your photo-finisher, ask for a Photo CD. Your film will be processed conventionally to produce negatives and a set of prints. Then, your film will be converted to a digital file, frame by frame, using a scanner. The scanned images are put into a high-speed computer for color and density corrections, and then placed on the compact disc. Each CD will hold about 100 images, and is packaged in a case with an index card showing each of the images recorded on that disc. If you had 24 exposures on your roll of film, return the CD with your next film processing and more images can be added to the CD. You will also usually save about $10 by supplying the CD yourself. Chapter 10 discusses working with Photo CDs in more detail.

Negatives, slides, or prints can also be scanned onto a Photo CD.

You can "play" or view the CD at home using a normal television set and a combination audio CD/Photo CD player. Computer

Today, a fax machine is a necessity.

users with CD-ROM XA drives can access the images directly. Current Photo CD players cannot be connected to computers. Photo CD (PCD) players look and operate like an Audio CD player but play Photo CDs on your television. They also play Audio CDs.

Photo CD technology is the storage system of the future.

### Office equipment

Will your business require a fax machine, telephone system, typewriter, photocopier, or label printer? Today, a fax machine is a necessity. If you can't afford a fax machine, a mailbox or office service business will look after outgoing and incoming fax transmissions for a small fee.

A photocopier is an expensive venture, unless you photocopy a lot of course manuals. A copier can be leased for $100 a month or more, depending on the features, or you can purchase an inexpensive one for under $1,000.

You may think typewriters are obsolete, but how do you plan to address envelopes? You could use your laser printer to output onto envelopes. How will you type onto mailing labels or large envelopes? You can purchase laser labels for your laser printer, purchase a label printer, or buy a typewriter.

## Internet Access

The Internet and the World Wide Web have made the biggest and fastest change in the computer industry. People want to get connected to the Internet to download information and solutions, as well as to post information and promotions about their own companies or services. The Internet also provides opportunities to designers who learn how to create interesting Web page designs for other businesses. You should be connected.

### Register with a local service provider

CompuServe, America Online, CRS Online, and Prodigy are popular service providers. Any local computer publication will have dozens of advertisements promoting service providers.

### Ask lots of questions

Before signing up with a service provider, ask lots of questions, including:

- How long has it been in business?

- How may users can it support at one time?

- How many network servers does it have?

- How much does it charge per month?

- How many staff members are available to assist users?

- Does it provide group accounts?

- How much connection time are you allowed before being billed extra, on top of the flat rate?

- Does it host business Web sites, and if so, how much does it charge?

- Can viewers access your site at any time? Some providers have more subscribers than they can handle, and viewers end up waiting to view your site or giving up because they cannot access it.

Chapter 12 discusses opportunities using the Internet in more detail.

## Ergonomics in the Office

### Working at the computer

Here are guidelines for maximizing your comfort while working at a computer:

- Top surface of the space bar on the keyboard should be no higher than 2 inches above the work space.

- While keying, the forearm and upper arm should form an angle of about 90 degrees, the upper arm almost vertical.

- The wrist should be relaxed and not bent. Wrist rests are recommended if the wrist is not supported.

- Keyboard should be directly in front of the operator.

- Top of screen should be eye level.

- Leave a large area free for documents and other work materials.

- Use an adjustable copy stand or document holder. Place it next to the screen, at the same height.

- Change the copy stand from one side of the screen to the other side periodically, so that neck muscles are not over-used. If you do a lot of typing, the copy stand should be directly in front of you, with the screen off to the side. This may reduce neck strain and pain.

QuarkXPress, Adobe PageMaker, Adobe InDesign, and Microsoft Publisher are the most popular page layout programs.

### Tips for avoiding eye strain

- Viewing distance of monitor should be 12" to 24".
- Screen should be free of glare or shadows from windows or lights.
- Images on screen should be sharp, easy to read, and shouldn't flicker.
- Light should shine on the copy, not the screen; adjustable lighting is recommended.
- Office interiors should be neutral colors, not too bright.
- Adjust screen brightness and contrast, so that images are brighter than the background screen. Be careful not to make it too bright.
- Clean the VDT screen regularly.

## Computer Software

After purchasing the hardware for a desktop publishing operation, you must choose software programs that will work with you to produce satisfactory results. Five years ago, desktop publishers were advised to buy a word processing program, a page layout program, and a graphics program, because each program had a specific job. Today, programs are much more powerful and are capable of doing more than one function. Sometimes one program will satisfy all your needs. Software programs are divided into ten categories:

### Page layout programs

QuarkXPress, Adobe PageMaker, Adobe InDesign, and Microsoft Publisher are the most popular page layout programs for designing publications, advertisements, stationery, business forms, and promotional materials. You can import text from a variety of programs, graphics, or scanned images and arrange them on a page.

Talk to your print shop before starting a project. You don't want to do a 12-page newsletter in Microsoft Publisher and then find out your print shop doesn't use that software and cannot output four-color separations to print your job.

### Graphics programs

Graphics or drawing programs are capable of transforming display type, creating logos, graphs, and illustrations. The most popular graphics programs are CorelDRAW!, Adobe Illustrator, and Macromedia FreeHand. Many clip art illustrations are created in Adobe Illustrator, so you can open them in a drawing program and alter them.

### Photo-editing programs

In the past few years, the popularity of photo-imaging software has skyrocketed as people alter photographs to achieve special effects or better reproduction. Adobe Photoshop, CorelPHOTO-PAINT!, and Macromedia Fireworks are common programs.

Adobe Photoshop is the most popular photo-imaging program because it allows you to remove stains and tears from photos, sharpen and retouch photos, adjust the brightness, contrast, or color of an image, mask and close cut photos, create stylized type and art, and perform prepress functions. There is a lot to the program to understand, so take a course to fully utilize its potential.

### Word processing programs

Type all documents longer than two pages in a word processor such as Microsoft Word, WordPerfect, or MacWrite. You could typeset directly into a page layout program, but a word processor will have a spell checker, grammar check, and thesaurus that are much more powerful. Most layout programs allow you to import a story into the layout from a word processing program.

### Multimedia or presentation programs

If you plan to produce multimedia, video editing, or electronic presentations, you will require additional software. Macromedia Director is the most popular multimedia program because you can add text, photos, video clips, sound, and interactive buttons to create an interactive or self-running presentation.

Adobe Premiere is a video-editing software program that allows you to digitize or edit video and sound clips. You can fade, flip, or slide from one video clip into a different one.

Microsoft PowerPoint, Macromedia Flash are presentation programs. You can create an electronic presentation to view on a computer screen or project onto a television or a large screen.

### Data base programs

A data base program is useful to maintain lists or create fill-in business forms. If you need to maintain a mailing list, a data base program will let you sort it alphabetically by name, by region, by postal code, or by other data. FileMaker Pro and FoxPro are good data base programs.

### Spreadsheet programs and accounting programs

Spreadsheet programs such as Lotus 1-2-3 and Microsoft Excel are excellent for recording numbers, producing tables and fill-in business forms, creating graphs, and setting up bookkeeping journals and ledgers.

AccPac Simply Accounting, MYOB (Mind Your Own Business), Multiledger, and Quicken are accounting programs that help you keep a set of books and produce financial statements for a business.

### Integrated programs

An integrated program combines several programs into one. ClarisWorks and Microsoft Works are a combination of word processing, graphics, data base, spreadsheet, and communications programs. Caution: these inexpensive programs are usually not as powerful as a designated program.

### Web design software

Web design software popularity has grown the most in the last ten years. Software programs such as Macromedia Dreamweaver, Microsoft FrontPage, and Adobe GoLive are popular Web page design programs that allow you to design a Web site and upload it to the Internet without knowing any HTML. Of course, there are still HTML programmers who love the challenge of writing their own HTML code and designing a Web page from scratch. Of course, you'll need a file transfer program such as Fetch to upload your Web site if you create it yourself.

If you would like to add animation and interactivity to your Web site, Macromedia Flash is a software program that allows you to do that.

### Miscellaneous programs and utilities

To maintain your computer or to have fun while computing, there are other programs such as Norton Utilities to diagnose and repair some computer problems, SAM virus check to check your hard drive and diskettes for viruses, and screen savers to protect your monitor.

## CHAPTER 7

# MARKETING YOUR BUSINESS

*You can't have a successful business if you keep it a secret.*

— BARBARA A. FANSON

In Chapter 2, we prepared a marketing plan to envision who our potential clients are. In this chapter, we'll discuss the best way to reach potential clients. Should you mail them a direct mail package? Or should you telephone them one at a time?

## Prospecting

Prospecting is the process of locating potential customers. A prospect is any organization or individual who has a need for your product or service. A lead is a name: an organization or individual who may turn out to be a prospect. A customer is an organization or individual who has already purchased your product or service.

## Networking

Two-thirds of my clients come from networking opportunities. I go to business functions, introduce myself, qualify potential clients, and speak knowledgeably about their publications or promotions. But I don't attend a meeting, trade show, class, or seminar empty-handed. Equipped with business cards and a 15-word summary of my business, I introduce myself with my name, my business's name, and the words "I specialize in …"

### Distribute business cards

Wearing a suit, I always keep my business cards in the left pocket so when I shake hands with my right hand, I can reach into my pocket for a business card. Giving the person my business card, he or she both hears and sees my name. The chances of remembering it are greater.

I place other people's business cards into my right pocket, so I don't get mine and theirs mixed up. When I leave a function, I write on the back where and when I received the business card and then I file it for future use.

If I'm talking to people and I realize I've forgotten their names, I can reach into my pocket and make a comment about their business cards. Actually, I'm memorizing their name.

I once attended a newsletter seminar presented by another business. I went because I knew that most of the attendees would be editors and there would be few designers. I was right. I was also given a list of all the attendees and their addresses. Within a week, they all got an introductory letter from me.

Stationary section discusses business cards in more detail.

### Qualifying a potential client

When I introduce myself to a potential client, I give a 15-word summary of my business. I watch to see how the person reacts; I can usually tell if he or she is interested. This is the first step to qualifying a potential client. Then, I ask questions about where that person works, his or her job function, who looks after publications, etc. If this person is not in a buying position, I move on. There's no use wasting either of our time.

To qualify a potential client, follow these four steps:

(a) Locate and contact the right people within the prospect organization.

(b) Meet with the right people.

(c) Probe to determine the prospect's needs.

(d) Develop a comprehensive strategy for converting the prospect into a customer.

You must sell "four levels to four levels." Your four levels are yourself, your business, your product or service concept, and your product or service. The prospect's four levels are the decision-maker, the influencer, the supervisor, and the user. The presentation is a formalized method of stating your case to the prospect. You have qualified the prospect once you define the criteria for winning the sale and the prospect agrees to accept that criteria.

## Opportunities exist everywhere

Opportunities to network exist everywhere. Two days after purchasing a computer, I met my biggest client while drinking coffee after church. I overheard someone say the word "computer" and I perked up as if he had said my name. I went over and introduced myself. He owned a marketing business and often used freelance writers and designers.

Another good opportunity came while I was instructing a night school computer class. An editor of a corporate full-color magazine was attending and asked me to quote on the project.

I have not had a promotion campaign for my desktop publishing business for three years, and yet, people still telephone me from out of the blue. Be aware of opportunities for meeting prospects in all situations you find yourself.

# Ask Existing Clients for Leads

If you already have satisfied clients, ask them if they know anyone else who might benefit from your service. Most newsletter editors know at least one other editor. Or, if you're producing a newsletter for the public relations department of a large company, the marketing department may also benefit from your services.

If you get leads — names of companies or individuals who could benefit from your service — telephone them to introduce yourself.

## Nine steps to successful sales calls

Sales professionals can make successful telephone calls to prospects by following these nine steps. Try these steps for a month and evaluate their effectiveness. You may need to adjust your methods.

- *Identify yourself.* For example, you might say, "Good morning. My name is _____ May I speak with Tom Smith?"

Be aware of opportunities for meeting prospects in all situations you find yourself.

- *Check person's availability to talk.* After repeating your name, ask, "Do you have a few moments to talk with me?"

- *Build a bridge.* Discuss something you have in common (friends, interests, activities) to build a friendship and trust. For example, "Michael Jones suggested we talk. He and I have worked together on several projects. How do you know Michael?"

- *Introduce sales message.* You might say something like, "The reason Michael thought I should call you is that he knows the work our firm does and thought we might be helpful to you. I can determine that, if you can take a minute to answer a few questions for me."

- *Fact finding.* Probe to determine the prospect's needs: "Michael says you produce a monthly newsletter. Tell me a little about your newsletter."

- *Sales message.* Continue with: "It sounds like you might need some assistance with it. I'm very experienced at producing newsletters. I recently helped a company with a newsletter similar to yours, and I'd be glad to talk with you about how I might assist you."

- *Address concerns or questions.* Answer questions briefly about your experience, the time required, how you could do it, fees, etc.

- *Gain commitment.* Suggest a meeting. Avoid asking questions that can be answered with a simple yes or no, such as, "Would you like to meet with me?" Instead, ask a question with two choices: "Perhaps we should get together and talk about this further. Would you prefer to meet on Tuesday or Thursday?" Instead of thinking about whether the prospect actually wants to meet with you, he or she is thinking about which would be better, Tuesday or Thursday.

- *Finish.* Discuss the kind of meeting, where, when, and who will be involved.

### Cold telephone sales calls

If you pick up a newsletter at a trade show, chances are there's a masthead inside with the editor's name and telephone number. Bingo! A lead! Why not telephone the editor to see if the editor does the production or uses a freelancer? Is the editor happy with the freelancer's work? You may have called at the right time. If the editor doesn't need your assistance right now, follow up by mailing an introductory letter or brochure.

I've had several people call me inquiring about possible work and I usually respond with "I don't need your help now, but send me your résumé and I'll keep it on file." They rarely follow through. And later, when I do need assistance, I don't have their names and telephone numbers, so I have to run an ad looking for someone. Don't let yourself be the one missing out on an opportunity.

Your business card should be a reflection of you and your expertise.

# Stationery

## Business cards

Your business card or envelope may be the first contact a potential client has with your business. It should be professional and establish an identity for you. Your business card should be a reflection of you and your expertise. A client may decide whether to work with you based on whether he likes the style of your artwork. If the client is conservative and your business card is outrageous, the client will immediately believe that you aren't capable of producing the look he or she wants.

As well, your name printed with black ink on a white card does not do you justice. Add a logo, symbol, or stylized type. Design and print your business card horizontally with a standard business card size of 3 ½" x 2".

## Letterhead

If you scan your logo into the computer, you can output letters and quotes with your logo. Since many quotes are faxed, you can save letterhead using this method. But you should have printed letterhead matching your business card, just in case. Since most documents are filed in folders or binders, use standard, letter-sized paper: 8 ½" x 11". Be sure to include your logo, business name, address, zip or postal code, telephone number, fax number, and any additional numbers so people can contact you.

Be sure to include your complete mailing address with zip or postal code to reduce payment delays.

## Envelopes

The no. 10 business envelope is the most popular size of envelope for mailing invoices, letters, newsletters, and promotional literature.

A no. 10 envelope is 9 ½" x 4 ⅛". Include your logo, business name, and return address on the top left-hand corner of the envelope. Telephone numbers are not printed on envelopes.

How will you address the envelope? Handwritten name and address? Typewritten name and address? You can purchase a label printer for your computer to produce one label at a time. If you're sending out several letters, add sheets of labels to your laser printer.

If you're sending out a lot of artwork in 9" x 12" envelopes or larger, you might want to create a mailing label.

### Diskette and envelope labels

Occasionally, you'll supply diskettes to clients, service bureaus, and associates. You can use your own preprinted labels or buy sheets of laser labels to use in your laser printer. Not only does it look more professional, but it also identifies where the disk originated, and what's on it.

Your diskette labels can also be used to address large envelopes that won't fit into a typewriter.

I produced my own mailing labels by outputting four on a letter-sized sheet of paper. I use tape to attach it to the envelope. A line of type at the bottom of the form reads "This label was attached with tape so you can re-use this envelope. It's our commitment to the environment." Not only are the labels practical, but my business looks good, too! And you can output as many as you want.

## Promotional Literature

If your freelance desktop publishing business wants to specialize in producing newsletters for other businesses, why not create your own promotional newsletter, brochure, or sales literature? Not only will a newsletter showcase your design skills but it is excellent to leave behind after talking to a potential client. It takes time to develop your own freelance business; newsletters are an effective form of promotion that will help speed it up.

Or, if you are making telephone sales calls to explore potential work opportunities, mail a self-promotional newsletter as a follow-up, whether you got the leads' business or not.

You could distribute your newsletters when attending networking functions, computer classes, seminars, or business meetings. If you get an opportunity to introduce yourself, give a 15-word summary of your business and hand out your newsletter.

Drop off a handful of newsletters when visiting print shops, service bureaus, or suppliers; they may have contacts who may be interested in your service. Mail newsletters to marketing or sales managers of local businesses.

If your self-promotional newsletter includes interesting, informative articles that businesspeople can use, they will probably save it. They may not need you right now, but they'll have a reminder of you when they do.

Most importantly, any form of literature promoting your business must be error free, well conceived, and attractive, or you are wasting your time and money.

Any form of literature promoting your business must be error free, well conceived, and attractive.

# *Advertising*

Should you run an advertisement in a publication you think your potential client will see? If it's the right market, try it.

## *Functions of advertising*

There are five functions of advertising. Which function will your ads perform?

### *Marketing*

- To identify products and differentiate them from those of competitors
- To communicate information about the product
- To induce the trial of new products by new users and to suggest repurchasing by existing users
- To stimulate a product's distribution
- To increase product use
- To build brand preference

### *Communications*

All forms of advertising communicate some message or information to a group of people. Whereas the marketing function deals more with promoting products, the communications function explains more about the business, its people, its product or service. What information do you want to reveal to the viewer of the ad?

### *Education*

People learn from advertising; they learn more about the products that are available to them, and they learn how the products can improve their lives.

### Economic

By making people aware of products, services, and ideas, advertising promotes sales. By informing many people at once about available products or services, advertising greatly reduces the cost of distribution and eases the task of personal selling. This leads to lower costs and higher profits.

### Social

Advertising has helped improve the standard of living in North America by publicizing the material, social, and cultural opportunities of a free enterprise, consumer society.

## How to create advertising that sells

A reader may spend five minutes reading a page in a magazine, or as little as 12 seconds scanning an entire two-page spread.

Trying to create an effective advertisement is very difficult today, since advertising is expensive and consumer buying habits have become more complex.

The four main objectives of an advertisement are AIDA:

- attract **attention** with color, size, motion, or illustration;
- arouse **interest** by explaining what the product or service can do for the reader;
- stimulate **desire** by making a reader want your product or service;
- lead to **action** by ending the body copy with "Don't delay call us today," or "Limited quantities," or "Send in this coupon today." You want the reader to act quickly and purchase your product or service.

Regardless of the medium used, advertisers should strive for continuity and resemblance between ads. Visual similarities such as the same border, format, style of photographs, or type style may help tie the ads together in advertising campaigns. And, it will help readers recognize your ads before they actually read them. Use a simple layout that will direct rather than confuse the reader. Avoid too many different typefaces and very decorative borders, as they may distract the reader or reduce the number of readers.

Illustrations, layout, and copy must work together to deliver the advertiser's sales message. Basic ad layouts include headline, illustration or photograph, body copy, logos, and signature (name of the company and address).

Five times more people read the headline than the body copy. The most effective headlines promise the reader a benefit: more miles to the gallon, less pimples, or super savings. A headline should capture attention and draw the reader into the ad. A headline can announce a new product, an improvement in an old product, or a new way to use an old product. Headlines that offer helpful information, such as "How to create advertising that sells," attract above average readership. To personalize the advertisement, add the brand name or the name of your city to the headline. Use a line or phrase that tells something significant: who, what, when, where, why are always good standbys.

Body copy should be concise, interesting, and to the point.

The illustration or photograph should depict the product or the sales event. A photograph of a forklift will immediately attract the attention of any reader interested in forklifts. To promote quality products, use quality photographs. If your photo is not sharp or has little contrast, it will not sell the product. Throw the photo away. Remember: your ad is a reflection of your business.

The body copy should describe consumer benefits and maintain the reader's interest. Be concise, interesting, and to the point. In most cases, complete sentences are easier to read than phrases or a few words. Avoid unusual words or difficult jargon, as your readers may misunderstand or become confused.

If the advertisement is promoting a brand new product, include the logo to help the reader recognize the brand. You can enhance the reputation of your business by featuring branded items.

The name, address, and logo of your business should be prominent and clean. This will help the reader locate your business.

Don't be afraid to mention prices; consumers over-estimate omitted prices.

I used to place small ads in the professional services section of *Marketing*, a *Maclean Hunter* magazine. It's distributed each week to advertising agencies and marketing firms. I used to promote my ability to write and produce newsletters. Each time the small ad ran, I got about eight phone calls, mostly inquiries about fees. Of the eight phone calls, I would get at least one project, which would pay for the ad, and then some.

## Direct Mail

Direct mail advertising is the term given to all forms of advertising sent directly to prospects through the postal service or private services. Direct mail ranks as the third most popular method of advertising among businesses, surpassed only by newspapers and television. Usually when a new business starts up, its first method of advertising is direct mail. The shortest distance between two points is a straight line: direct mail offers the "straightest" line to the desired prospect.

Check in your Yellow Pages for listings of direct mail houses.

## Introductory and Follow-up Letters

### Introductory letter

An effective introductory letter is your prospective client's first impression of your business. Keep your letter brief and to the point. Be specific about the kind of work you think this client will need from you. State your qualifications for this type of work. Mention your top clients by name. Include awards or special recognition. Enclose a clipping or other short promotional item. Let the client know you will follow up by calling for an appointment for a meeting. Use your business stationery. Sample 1 shows an example of an introductory letter.

### Follow-up letter

The follow-up letter usually follows a telephone sales call, networking function, or chance meeting. It reminds the recipient of your discussion and mentions your name once more. The more potential clients hear or see your name, the more they'll remember it when something comes up. Sample 2 illustrates a typical follow-up letter.

### Confirmation letter

You should confirm the project, the payment terms, and the total in writing to protect yourself in case of late or insufficient payment. A confirmation letter does not need to be filled with legal jumbo. Just restate the terms of the verbal agreement in everyday language. Describe as closely as possible exactly what the client will be getting. If a client balks or implies that such a letter illustrates a lack of trust on your part, explain that the confirmation letter is simply a way for you to keep track of ongoing projects and the client's specifications. Sample 3 is an example of a confirmation letter.

## Public Relations Tools

The tools of communication that a PR person can use are varied, from brochures to newsletters to audio/visual materials. PR materials are produced in much the same way as advertising with emphasis on writing, art, layout, and production.

### Press release

A press release is a typewritten sheet of information (usually 8½" x 11") sent to print and broadcast outlets to generate publicity. Information may include the announcement of a new product, promotion of an executive, or the signing of a union contract.

### Press kit

A press kit is used to gain publicity at staged events such as press conferences or open houses. It includes a basic fact sheet detailing the event, a list of the participants, brochures prepared for the event, a news story for the broadcast media, and news and feature stories for the print media.

Photographs of events, products in use, new equipment, or newly promoted executives lend interest to an otherwise dull news story.

### Booklets, brochures, pamphlets, and books

Printed materials are used extensively in public relations work. Internal materials can inform employees of new training methods, health issues, a history of the company, and a host of other things.

### Letters, inserts, and enclosures

Letters, written on behalf of the company, can be sent out to customers, suppliers, retailers or editors. Inserts or enclosures may be included with an invoice to explain a rate increase or special sale.

### Annual report

An annual report is a formal document issued by a corporation to its stockholders and is a reflection of the corporation's condition at the close of the business year.

### House organs and newsletters

While a house organ is an internal company publication, a newsletter can be distributed to prospects, suppliers, and clients. A well-produced newsletter can promote goodwill, increase sales, or mold public opinion.

**Sample 1**
**Introductory Letter**

# THE STUDIO

869 Main Street E
Pleasantville, State 23456

January 2, 200-

Jane Doe
The Client's Office
123 Any Street
Anytown, State 12345

Dear Ms. Doe:

We are interested in helping The Client's Office with the design and writing of its bi-weekly newsletter, and with other communication assignments.

The Studio is a network of designers and writers who do a range of corporate communication work: newsletters, advertising, sales literature, corporate identity programs, and corporate and product brochures. Our clients include MM Telephone, Sterling Education Center, Marsh TV, Coco Paving, Juniper College, Industrial Magazine, Sport and Co., and many others.

Our accounts are varied, but we are particularly experienced with newsletters, because we have done so many over the years. We would like to meet you and show you some of our work.

I have been in the graphic design industry since 1978 as a graphic designer, typographer, advertising sales representative, and camera operator. With the evolution of electronic typesetting and layout, I have become excited about desktop publishing and its seemingly endless possibilities. Understandably, more emphasis has to be placed on the ability of the graphic designer to unite traditional methods of typesetting and paste-up with current electronic composition.

I believe The Studio has skills that can be helpful to The Client's Office, and I will call you soon to see if we can arrange to show you our portfolio. Even if you have no immediate needs, it might be useful for you to see what we're capable of. To give you more information about us, I'm enclosing an article that appeared recently in *Computer Dealer News*.

Yours truly,

Barbara A. Fanson
President and Production Manager

## Sample 2
## Follow-up Letter

**THE STUDIO**

869 Main Street E
Pleasantville, State 23456

January 2, 200-

Jane Doe
The Client's Office
123 Any Street
Anytown, State 12345

Dear Ms. Doe:

Thank you for meeting with me yesterday so that I could present myself and my business.

As I mentioned during our discussion, I have been in the graphic arts field since 1978 as a graphic designer, typesetter, paste-up artist, and camera operator. I graduated from Fanshawe College with a Diploma in Graphic Design in 1981. During the last few years I have been involved in the desktop publishing evolution by taking courses at George Brown and Centennial colleges.

I would like you to consider The Studio for your next promotional project for two reasons:

- I am trained in the traditional methods of typesetting and paste-up, as well as today's electronic composition;
- I can provide project management from concept through editorial, production, printing, and distribution.

At The Studio, we can assist clients in the planning and implementation of a variety of contemporary communications. The company has successfully completed projects in the areas of advertising, newsletter, promotion, direct mail, corporate identification, editorial design, and corporate/product brochures for such clients as: *Jack's Electronics, Marsh TV*, MM Telephone, Sterling Education Centre, Juniper College, Industrial Magazine, Sport and Co., Coco Paving.

I am looking forward to working with you,


Barbara A. Fanson

President and Production Manager

**Sample 3**
**Confirmation Letter**

# THE STUDIO
869 Main Street E
Pleasantville, State 23456

February 4, 200-


Jane Doe
The Client's Office
123 Any Street
Anytown, State 12345

Dear Ms. Doe:

It was a pleasure speaking with you on April 4 about designing a company logo. It is my understanding that I will supply you with film for the logo by June 31, 200-, and that I will receive a total of $900 for this work, half payable now and half due 30 days after I deliver the finished design. I look forward to working with you.


Yours truly,



Barbara A. Fanson
President and Production Manager

## Write an Article for Other Publications

Another way to promote your freelance writing business is to write articles for other publications: newspapers, magazines, and trade journals. If you want to specialize in writing and laying out newsletters, why not write an article for a magazine or community newspaper about the benefits of newsletters? You could supply the article at no charge to the publication, in exchange for an extended byline at the end of the article.

Your article about newsletters could mention how they are an excellent form of promotion for companies. Remember, the objective of this newsletter article is to obtain business clients who may be interested in using a newsletter as a form of promotion.

Many publications love having writers submit articles. Contact the editor of the publication in advance with your article idea and ask him or her if a photo or illustration would be helpful. Promptly follow up your telephone conversation with a confirmation and thank-you letter.

Press releases containing vital information, rather than heavy promotional copy, are an excellent way to spread the word. Create a news article or press release mentioning how you specialize in newsletters because they help businesses promote themselves. Many publications will run press releases because they are informative or add filler material.

## Use the Internet to Promote Your Business

There are many ways that you can use the Internet to promote your own desktop publishing business:

- Design a Web site for your own business and upload it so that you'll gain experience on how the process actually works. You'll find out how long it takes to design a page or animation, which may help you establish a fee for your service. Having your own Web site lets potential clients see the type of work that you can do for them. A potential client can see if your Web site is well-designed, functional, or whether it has special effects.

- Register with major search engines such as Excite, Yahoo, or Google. There are over 400 search engines. Choose 10 to 25 keywords to describe your service or product and go to a search engine's Web site and look for a link such as Register

Your Web site or Submit a Site and fill in their online form.

- Consider registering a domain name that is easy for potential clients to remember and easy for you to promote on your printed stationery and in advertisements. For example, <www.sterlinged.com> is easier to remember and say on the telephone than <www.sterling@aibn.on.com>. Besides, why promote the Internet service provider on your promotions?

- Consider custom e-mail addresses for your business. Use a catchy word to describe your service such as <learn@sterlinged.com> or <action@sterlinged.com>.

- Include your Web site address on all promotions, stationery, signage, and advertisements. People use the Internet for obtaining more information about a company or person.

- Trade a banner ad with another business. You could have a small banner ad on someone else's Web site and in exchange they would have a banner ad on your Web site. When you trade banner ads, remember that you and the other business should offer complimenting services; for example, a desktop publisher could trade banner ads with a local print shop, writer, or photographer.

- Purchase a banner ad on a search engine or directory. For example, a banner ad on Yahoo's Web site would be around $26 CPM (Cost Per Thousand) page view for a run of Yahoo Web site, where ads rotate through the pages.

## E-mail Promotions

Electronic-mail promotions (e-mail) used to be an effective method of promoting your services or products, but today, people are receiving over 100 e-mail messages daily and yours may be deleted along with other SPAM e-mails.

If you are planning to e-mail potential clients, consider an e-newsletter that provides information rather than a flyer that will be deleted instantly. A well-written and well-designed electronic newsletter may make a slower trip to the waste basket. Include useful information that a client could benefit from and may even want to save or print for future information. Don't forget to include a link from your e-mail to your Web site.

CHAPTER **8**

# PROJECT PROCEDURES

*You can't lose sight of your goals. If you focus on becoming a winner, you'll do whatever it takes to become one.*

— FRANK FERRERA

It's important that you record how much time is spent on each project, the cost of outside expenses, and that you know what stage each project is in. Business guidelines determine the way your business operates. Procedure is the step-by-step method of working to implement the business guidelines. What steps are needed to get the job done? You need to set up a routine for handling activities such as client consultation, scheduling the various steps of the project, getting approval of your work, dealing with printers, and collecting your fee.

## Obtain Information about the Project

Meet with the client or discuss the project on the telephone. Fill out a client information sheet (Sample 4) for first-time clients so that you understand the client's products, services, and objectives. Make sure you clearly understand what the project requires and your role in the project. This form can be filled out once and filed away for future reference. There is no need to complete one for each project.

Complete the production order form (Sample 5) so you have the information in writing and signed by the client.

## Prepare an Agreement

Filling out an agreement of terms and conditions (Sample 6) is essential for first-time clients. Once you have established a relationship with a client and you know how they pay, you may not need to prepare an agreement. Notice that the sample agreement includes both the client's name (the contact person you're dealing with) and the name of the company he or she represents. Make sure you file this agreement in a safe place for at least one year.

## Open a Job Docket

A job docket is an envelope (often 9" x 11" envelopes are large enough) in which you keep all paperwork, documents, artwork, etc., for that particular job. The job docket form (Sample 7) could be taped, stapled, or printed on to the side of the envelope. You could also use a production order or time sheet as a job docket form.

I carry job dockets in my briefcase to store any diskettes, copy, photos, or artwork the client gives me. The envelope ensures that I keep everything together and that the client can see I'm organized. As well, if you have to take legal action to collect payment from a client, all the evidence has been stored in the job docket.

After the job is completed and has been invoiced, file the job docket alphabetically in a filing cabinet.

## Establish a Production Schedule

Who will do what, what are reasonable deadlines, and will you require outside suppliers, such as writers, photographers, illustrators, printers, service bureaus, or direct mail houses?

The production schedule form (Sample 8) is useful for scheduling the time required to complete the project and to make sure you'll meet the deadline. Give the client two copies to sign: one to return to you, the other to retain in his or her files. How much time is required for each stage of the project?

## Contact Suppliers

Call suppliers (writers, photographers, illustrators, printers, service bureaus, or direct mail houses) to discuss your needs and to obtain a quotation for their services. You might want to fax a printing bid request (Sample 9) to printers.

While discussing the project with your commercial printer, ask how the printer would like the artwork supplied: on disk, output onto paper, or output onto film. Should you assemble the pages into printer's spreads or should you gang several small items onto one page? What line screen will be used to produce halftones? Chapter 11 includes more information about dealing with printers and suppliers.

## Prepare a Quotation

Once you have gathered estimates from outside vendors, you can prepare a price estimate worksheet (Sample 10) to calculate how much it will cost to complete the project. Then, prepare a formal quotation (Sample 11) for the client.

## Discuss Fee, Schedule, and General Concepts With The Client

Before proceeding any farther, you want to make sure first-time clients know how much the project will cost them and how long it should take you to complete the project, assuming there are no additional changes.

## Begin Working on the Project

As you work on the project, keep track of the time spent and any expenses incurred that can be billed to the client. Use a time sheet (Sample 12) to record time spent on the project, and expenses incurred for it. Periodically, fill out a project summary form (Sample 13) to fax to the client to keep him or her informed on the progress. A project summary form is essential for long-term assignments, especially if you're expecting to get paid in installments along the way. For small assignments, I usually don't fill out a project summary form, but I do keep clients informed by telephone.

Make sure first-time clients know how much the project will cost them and how long it should take to complete.

## CONVERTING FILES FROM ONE
## COMPUTER PLATFORM TO ANOTHER

Client Marianne uses WordPerfect on an MS-DOS comput-er to write her stories. Designer Barbara uses QuarkXPress on a Macintosh computer to lay out the pages. How do they get an article from one computer platform to anoth-er? Here are six ways to cross platforms:

1. Client faxes story to designer who re-types story into own computer.

2. Client mails story to designer who uses a desktop scanner with optical character recognition software to scan the story into the computer. The scanned story is opened up into a word processing program and spell checked. Sometimes the OCR software will change an "O" to a "0" or an "S" to a "5."

3. Client ships diskette or CD to designer and designer tries to import the file directly into QuarkXPress. Most page layout programs can import word-processed documents from Microsoft Word, WordPerfect, and other programs. The writer can also save the word processing file as a ASCII text file, which page layout programs can import. **Caution:** Newer Macintosh computers do not have a diskette drive, so save it on a CD. You may want to discuss file types with the designer before sending them. And don't stuff or zip a file for someone on a different computer platform.

4. Client ships/takes diskette to a service bureau for data conversion, making sure to supply a blank diskette so he or she is not charged extra.

5. Client sends story by e-mail or modem to designer. Both parties must have an Internet connection.

6. If a page layout program won't import a story typed on a different computer platform, try opening story in a word processing program on a Macintosh com-puter before bringing it into a page layout program.

At this time, I also prepare a sample style sheet (Sample 14) for first-time clients, displaying which type size and font will be used for headlines, body text, cutlines, etc. I either fax it to the client or meet with the client to review the preliminary layouts and draft copy.

It is also a good idea to keep a style sheet on hand should you be away and need another desktop publisher to cover for you. Sample 14 is the style sheet for this book.

## Supervise Photo Shoot/Taping Session

If photos are required, arrange a photographer, products, or models. Be sure to have models complete a model release (Sample 15) that grants you permission to use their image in your artwork.

If you are having a video or music prepared for a multimedia project, make sure you have the right to use the recording on this project and future assignments.

## Complete Artwork

Once you have all the photos, copy, and artwork, you can assemble them in a page layout program. If the client is supplying the copy on a disk, you may have to clean up the disk by deleting extra spaces or returns. Sample 16 is a list of some of the tasks the client can do to help save you time when working with electronic files he or she has supplied. Give your client a copy of this list once you have determined that the client will be supplying you with electronic files. The list is also handy for you to follow as you clean up client-supplied electronic files.

## Proofread

After completing the artwork, output it on your laser printer. Proofread the laser output carefully using the proofreading checklist (see Checklist 1).

Proofreading involves checking the detail, meaning, spelling, and grammar of a document. Never rely on the spell check or grammar check that comes with your software program. Always output a copy to proofread. One time I wanted to typeset "tips to help run your business." I accidentally typeset "tips to help ruin your business." It passed the spell check and the grammar check.

### Checklist 1
### Proofreading Checklist

☐ Check each page and reference number carefully.

☐ Double-check all other numbers.

☐ Mistakes tend to be clustered, so if you find one, look for others around it.

☐ Make sure the information is in the right sequence.

☐ Notice paragraph lengths; note when they're too long (shorter is better).

☐ Check to see if page and section references are accurate.

☐ Check spelling.

☐ Check grammar.

☐ Be sure that brackets, quotations, and parentheses are used correctly.

☐ Check punctuation.

☐ Watch for repeated words, such as "the the."

☐ Look for missing punctuation, such as commas or periods.

☐ Look for missing words (often small ones such as "a" or "the" are left out).

Read each letter of each word. Read each word. Read the sentence and make sure it makes sense. Sometimes the only error is a misplaced word or an omitted word, but the meaning can be changed drastically.

It is best to work on a flat surface or drafting table with good lighting. Use a colored pencil, pen, or marker. Use the straight edge of a ruler or card to guide your eye along. Have several reference books handy, including a good dictionary, a secretary's manual, and a thesaurus.

Proofreaders use symbols to indicate errors or omissions. After the text is proofread, it is returned to the typesetter for corrections. When the text is perfect, it is forwarded to the next step in the production cycle.

If you're not sure how to execute trapping, ask your service bureau how much it would charge for this service.

## Get Client Approval

Show or fax the laser proofs to the client for his or her approval. Make sure the client signs and dates the proof or completes the proofing approval checklist (Sample 17). Once you get past this stage in the production cycle, it becomes more expensive to make changes, so make sure the client approves the work done so far.

After making the client's changes, output another laser proof to make sure that every change was implemented and that the text didn't re-flow. If there were numerous changes and time permits, ask the client to check it once more. Always have the client sign and date a proof as it relieves you of the responsibility should something go wrong.

## Produce Mechanicals

In the traditional graphic arts industry, the next stage would be the mechanical stage — preparing the artwork for the printing process. The mechanical stage or prepress stage includes trapping, color separations, and imagesetting. A service bureau or large print shop can output your file on an imagesetter rather than a laser printer. An imagesetter is a machine with at least 1,270 dots per inch, rather than 300 or 600 dpi as on your laser printer, so the quality will be much better. (Service bureaus are discussed in more detail in Chapter 11.) If you're not sure how to execute trapping on a computer, ask your service bureau or print shop how much it would charge for this service.

## Proof Mechanicals and Get Client Approval

A service bureau or print shop can produce blueline proofs, color overlay proofs, or color laminated proofs from the final film before the printing stage. This provides another opportunity to check the project before it actually goes on press. A blueline proof, sometimes called a dylux, is a sheet of light-sensitive paper exposed with the film. This yellow and blue proof can be checked to make sure everything is in the proper position. A color overlay proof, also called a color key, has an overlay for each color of ink to be used. A color laminated proof, also called a match print, has the color overlays laminated, so you can't lift them. Most printers will not print a four-color job without first seeing a color proof. Have a proof made from the film and have your client check it once more.

---

**TIPS FOR CHECKING COLOR PROOFS**

(a) Repetitive backgrounds

If a common color or tint background is required for several pages in a newsletter, it may be difficult to maintain consistency across pages. For example, if a buff color is used in the background, it may consist of a percentage tint of process yellow. If some pages require a heavy weight of yellow to be run for the photos, the tints on those pages will be heavier than on the other pages. A special fifth color (a Pantone color) for the backgrounds only should prevent this problem. Remember, it is more expensive to run five colors than four.

(b) Mechanical tints

When specifying tints, give percentages of the process colors, which can be obtained from a tint chart. For example, specify 100 percent magenta and 100 percent yellow to create red. Avoid specifying tints with a Pantone color swatch or reference number to match, as many special colors cannot be obtained from the four-color process.

The tint on the proof can be checked against the tint chart. Check the proofs for mottled tints, which can be caused by the film or plate being exposed out of contact. Watch for moiré, an undesirable pattern

---

created when reproductions are made from halftones.

(c) Color bar

The color bar on the side of a process color page compares the amount of color used in the film and how much is used in the printing process. For example, if the proofer has used too much yellow ink, so that the proof looks too yellow even though the film is correct, the color bar will show this.

(d) Register

Check registration marks to see if the job has been proofed in register. If it is correct, all you will see is black. If it is out of register, the colors will show next to the black.

(e) Trim and bleed

Check trim marks for position and that the bleed allowance is correct.

(f) Flopping

When a photo or illustration appears reversed left to right in a color proof, it should be marked "flop." This correction requires more than just turning the film over, because the emulsion would be on the wrong side and therefore out of contact with the plate. A new contact film should be made with the emulsion on the correct side.

(g) Fit

If the register marks fit, but you can see colors sticking out from the edge of the picture, the job has been planned out-of-fit.

The only purpose of blueline, overlay, or laminated proofs is to compare them to your laser proofs. You do not want to make changes at this stage. Any change you make will be expensive since you'll have to go back and correct it on the computer, output new film, and make a new proof. Circle or mark anything directly on the blueline and write on it how it is to be fixed. Checklist 2 will help you check the proofs. Make any necessary changes and have new film output.

For new clients, I often ask for a 50 percent deposit before printing.

## Deliver Film and Proofs to Printer

After the client has approved the film proofs, take the film and the proofs to your commercial printer. Protect yourself by filling out the printing instructions form (Sample 18). A printer may not remember everything you say, so supply written instructions. At the very minimum, specify the quantity, ink colors, paper stock and color, and finishing operations.

Usually, the printer will give you the invoice, which you can mark up and resell to the client at a slightly higher price. For very large runs or expensive jobs, you may prefer to have the client pay the printer directly so you don't have to pay a large printing bill before the client pays you. For new clients, I often ask for a 50 percent deposit before printing and the balance on delivery.

## Do a Press Check

When you take the film to the printer, a printing plate will be made for the press. There will be a plate for each color. The job will then be scheduled for press. If it is a large, color run, you may want to be present for a press check. If you arrange to check your printed piece on the press, you must go once the press telephones you to come. Checklist 3 lists things to look for when doing a press check.

Once the project has been printed, evaluate the print job. Chapter 11 discusses this in more detail.

## Deliver Printed Material to the Client

The next step is determining how the printed material will be delivered to the client. Will the printer ship it? Or will you pick it up and deliver it? Will the client pick it up from the printer? Will the printed material fit in your car? The printer may charge you for shipping, which you can charge back to the client. If I deliver the job to the client, I usually charge a nominal amount for delivery.

## Invoice the Client

Use the time sheet (Sample 12) to add up the time spent on the project and record it on the project billing worksheet (Sample 19). Any invoices you received from outside suppliers and other expenses should be marked up and recorded on the project billing worksheet. A typical markup is 10 percent to 20 percent. Use the project billing worksheet to prepare an invoice (Sample 20).

## Checklist 2
## Proof Checklist

- [ ] Is the type sharp?
- [ ] Are there any broken characters?
- [ ] Is any type missing or in the wrong place?
- [ ] Is everything squared and centered as it should be?
- [ ] Are photos and art cropped correctly?
- [ ] Are photos in the right spots?
- [ ] Do photos butt up against the frame as they are supposed to?
- [ ] Are there any marks, specs, flaws, or flecks on the blueline? Circle all.
- [ ] Is anything missing?
- [ ] Is anything there that's not supposed to be there?
- [ ] Is the size right?
- [ ] Are the folds correct? Try folding it to make sure.
- [ ] Is the registration accurate?
- [ ] Are color breaks right?
- [ ] How is the color alignment?
- [ ] Do colors butt up against each other accurately?
- [ ] Are the colors where they're supposed to be?

**TIP:** Place the proof on top of the laser print on a light table. This method helps spot type that is missing or has reflowed.

## Checklist 3
## Press Checklist

☐ Have the changes and corrections you made on a blueline or color overlay proof been carried out as specified?

☐ Is your job being printed on the right paper?

☐ Is the sheet absolutely clean? There should be no specks in either the inked or uninked areas.

☐ How is the ink density?

☐ Are solid areas consistently solid?

☐ Is the registration accurate?

☐ Is the black ink, black enough?

☐ Are the colors right?

My invoices are generated in FileMaker Pro, a data base program, so I can automatically update my mailing list. The invoices are very efficient. When I create a new invoice, it's sequentially numbered and dated. Mathematical functions are also automated. Formulas are used to calculate the sales tax and the total amount. The form also has pop-up menus so I can choose the appropriate pretyped sentence.

I usually output three copies of the invoice on my laser printer. Two copies are mailed to the client and one copy is filed in the front section of a binder. These are my unpaid invoices. Once an invoice is paid, I write the date the payment was received on my copy and file it in the back of the binder in the paid section.

When you complete the deposit slip for your bank, record the invoice number on your copy of the deposit slip so you'll have a reference. Make sure to write on the back of the check "for deposit only, your company name" and your account number.

## Review the Project

After you've finished the project, and the invoice has been sent off in the mail to the client, take some time to review the project. Did you make money on it? Were there things that could have been handled differently? Is there anything you would change the next time you do a similar project? It's a good idea to review and analyze a completed project so you can improve it in the future. Write notes on the job docket that you can refer to later. I also record the invoice number and fee on the job docket so I'll know at a glance how much to charge next time.

## File the Project

Once the invoice has been sent to the client and the printed material has been delivered to the client, you can file the project. Organization is the key to finding this project later, should the client decide to use it again.

While working on a project, it is a good idea to save the electronic file on the computer and back it up onto another disk. A hard drive will process the information faster than a diskette or other removable media cartridge. Once the project is finished, you can archive the electronic file.

After completing a project, you could burn the electronic file onto a compact disc (CD) and deliver it to the print shop or film house. When the print shop has finished printing the project, you should always ask for the CD back so you can file it away. You can either store the CD in the Job Docket and file it alphabetically in a filing cabinet or number the CDs and file them separately from the Project Docket. Write down the number of the CD on the Project Docket. The CDs can be numerically organized after you write down everything that is on the CD on the case cover. Don't forget to save all logos and images on the CD so the complete project is saved together.

The paperwork is saved in a job docket or large 9" x 12" envelope and filed in a regular filing cabinet. The job docket contains all the information: two printed samples, the laser proofs, client information, price estimate worksheet, quotation, agreement, production schedule, project summary, time sheet, sample style sheet, photo/video/audio release, printing quotes, and the project billing worksheet. It's important to save this information for several years in case you're audited by the government or you have to go after the client for payment.

## Sample 4
## Client Information Sheet

Client name: _____

Company represented: _____

Address: _____

City: _____ State/Prov.: _____ Zip/P.C.: _____

Telephone: _____ Fax: _____

E-mail address: _____

What is the nature of the client's business? _____

How long has the company been in business? _____

Who are its competitors? _____

What does the client expect from you? _____

_____

Has the client ever used designers before? If so, in what capacity? _____

_____

What type of project does this client require? _____

_____

What does the client expect to accomplish with this project? _____

_____

What are the client's personal goals in this business? _____

_____

Project description: _____

_____

_____

_____

## Sample 5
## Production Order Form

Client: _____

Company represented: _____

Date: _____

Project name: _____

Project description: _____

_____

_____

_____

Project objectives: _____

_____

_____

_____

Price estimate total: _____

Due date: _____

Schedule: _____

_____

_____

Special information: _____

_____

_____

_____

Client authorization signature to begin work: _____

Date: _____

## Sample 6
## Agreement of Terms and Conditions

Client name: _____

Company represented: _____

Address: _____

City: _____ State/Prov.: _____ Zip/P.C.: _____

Telephone: _____ Fax: _____

Project name: _____

Project description: _____

1. The total cost for this project is estimated at:_____(see estimate).

2. All expenses incurred to complete this order are the responsibility of the client.

3. On receipt of full payment, the designer grants the client the following rights in the designs:


    All rights not explicitly granted in the agreement remain the exclusive property of the designer. Unless otherwise specified, the designer retains ownership of all original artwork, whether preliminary or final, and the client will return such artwork within sixty (60) days after use.

4. Payment for this project will be made according to the following schedule:


5. Payment for all invoices are due:

6. Designer fees quoted apply only to regular working hours: 9 a.m. to 5 p.m., Monday through Friday. If the client requests that project work be performed at times other than the stipulated office hours, additional overtime fees of $ _____ per hour will be charged, except for corrections made necessary by the designer.

7. All costs are estimates only. Any alterations by the client may result in price changes.

8. All additional costs that exceed the original estimate will be quoted to the client, in writing, before the costs are incurred.

9. The designer does not have the authority to exceed this estimate without client approval.

10. The terms and conditions of this agreement are valid for thirty (30) days only.

11. The designer's ability to meet the requirements of the production order and production schedule depends on the client delivering the material on time.

12. If the project is canceled at any time, the client is responsible for all expenses incurred to that point.

13. If a dispute arises between the designer and client over any term or condition agreed to in this agreement, the client will be subject to pay all reasonable attorney's fees if the dispute requires legal counsel.

I have agreed to the terms and conditions presented in this agreement as it applies to the project named and described above.

Client signature: _____ Date: _____

# PROJECT DOCKET

Project _____

Client: _____

Bill to: _____          Date Ordered : _____          Date Required : _____

Address: _____          Project Desciption: _____

City, Prov.: _____

Contact: _____          Position: _____

Telephone: _____          Fax: _____

## ADVERTISING

Ad Name: _____          Issue: _____

Publication: _____          Mat'l Deadline: _____

Space Deadline: _____          Phone: _____

Media Rep.: _____          Phone: _____

Production Rep.: _____

Size: _____          Colour: _____          Price: _____

☐ Artboard ☐ Neg. Film ☐ Contact ☐ Dupe ☐ Lino

## PRINTING

Name: _____          Quantity: _____

No. of Pages: _____          1 or 2 sides: _____

Ink Colour(s): _____

Stock: _____          Colour: _____

Bindery: _____

Printer: _____          Quotation: _____

Contact: _____          Telephone: _____

### TIME SHEET

| Date | Description | Code | Time | Cost |
|------|-------------|------|------|------|
|      |             |      |      |      |
|      |             |      |      |      |
|      |             |      |      |      |
|      |             |      |      |      |

### OUTSIDE SUPPLIES

| Date | Description | Actual | Cost |
|------|-------------|--------|------|
|      |             |        |      |
|      |             |        |      |
|      |             |        |      |

### QUOTATIONS

| Date | From | Actual | Cost |
|------|------|--------|------|
|      |      |        |      |
|      |      |        |      |

### INVOICED

| Date | No. | Price |
|------|-----|-------|
|      |     |       |
|      |     |       |

Project: _____

Project number: _____

Name/description: _____

_____

**Stage 1: Concept — Due date**

Client meeting: _____

Concept development: _____

Contact subs/vendors: _____

Estimates from subcontractors: _____

Project estimate: _____

Design: _____

Copy: _____

Editing: _____

Revisions: _____

Client approval: _____

_____

_____

_____

**Stage 2: Production — Due date**

Layout: _____

Client approval: _____

Comprehensive: _____

Client approval: _____

Copy revisions: _____

Client approval: _____

Trapping/color seps.: _____

Blueline/color proofs: _____

Client approval: _____

Revisions: _____

Artwork to printer: _____

Press approval: _____

Delivery to client: _____

Client signature: _____ Date: _____

*Please sign both copies. Retain one for your file and return the other to us.*

## Sample 9
## Printing Bid Request

*Your logo here*

Printing company: _____ Contact person: _____

Address: _____

Tel.: _____ Fax: _____

Project number: _____ Project description: _____

_____

_____

### Printing specifications

Quantity: _____ Number of sides: _____

Print size: _____ Finished size: _____

Paper color: _____

Paper stock: _____

No. of colors: _____ PMS ink no.: _____ Varnish:_____

Bleeds:_____ Screens:_____ Reverses: _____

Halftones: _____ Film: _____ Separations:_____

Proofs/blueline: _____ Overlay: _____ Laminated: _____

Bindery/fold: _____ Drill: _____ Score: _____

Die cut: _____ Perforations: _____ Emboss: _____

Other: _____

Pack: _____ Mailing:_____

Mailing instructions:_____

Delivery instructions: _____

Date due: _____ Please return bid by: _____

## Sample 10
## Price Estimate

Client: _____  Project number: _____

Project name/description: _____

_____

| Production | Time | Cost/hour | Total production cost |
|---|---|---|---|
| Client meetings: | | | |
| Research: | | | |
| Concept development: | | | |
| Organization: | | | |
| Layout/design: | | | |
| Art direction: | | | |
| Illustration: | | | |
| Type mark-up: | | | |
| Production: | | | |
| Consulting with suppliers: | | | |
| Copywriting/editing: | | | |
| Proofing: | | | |
| Press approvals: | | | |
| Account administration: | | | |
| Other: | | | |

**Printing prices**

| Quantity | Price | Mark-up | Client's price |
|---|---|---|---|
| | | | |
| | | | |
| | | | |

**Sub-contractor/supplier prices**

| Service | Price | Mark-up | Client's price |
|---|---|---|---|
| Photography: | | | |
| Typesetting: | | | |
| Film/camera supplies: | | | |
| Other: | | | |

## Sample 11
## Quotation

Date: _____

Project: _____    Project number: _____

Client: _____    Company represented: _____

Project description: _____

_____

| Production | Estimated time | Cost per hour | Estimated production cost |
|---|---|---|---|
| Research | | | |
| Concept | | | |
| Layout | | | |
| Consult with vendors | | | |
| Photography | | | |
| Copy/articles | | | |
| Scanning | | | |
| Art/illustrations | | | |
| Page layout | | | |
| Imagesetting | | | |
| Film proofs | | | |
| Printer | | | |
| Press approvals | | | |
| Finishing operations | | | |
| Distribution | | | |
| Account administration | | | |

**Printing prices**

**Quantity**                    **Price**

_____

_____

*Please note: This is an estimate only and is subject to change should specifications change. This estimate is valid for three months. Client-requested changes will be billed additionally.*

**Client approval**: _____

**Contractors/outside suppliers**

**Service**                    **Price**

Photography _____

Writing/editing _____

Proofreading _____

Imagesetting _____

Other _____

Total estimated cost _____

Date: _____

*Sample 12*
*Time Sheet*

| Client _____ | | Project _____ | | | | |
|---|---|---|---|---|---|---|
| **Date** | **Description** | **Time** | **Meeting** | **Typeset** | **Layout** | **Other** |
| | | | | | | |
| | | | | | | |
| | | | | | | |
| | | | | | | |
| | | | | | | |
| | | | | | | |
| | | | | | | |
| | | | | | | |
| | | | | | | |
| | | | | | | |
| | | | | | | |
| | | | | | | |
| | | | | | | |
| | | | | | | |
| | | | | | | |
| | | | | | | |
| | | | | | | |
| | | | | | | |
| | | | | | | |
| | | | | | | |
| | | | | | | |
| | | | | | | |
| | | | | | | |

## Sample 13
## Project Summary

Date: _____ Project: _____ Project number: _____

Client: _____ Company represented: _____

Address _____

City: _____ State/Prov.: _____ Zip/P.C.: _____

Telephone: _____ Fax: _____

Project description: _____ Total hours to date: _____

Things on hold: _____

We are waiting for client approval on: _____

Recommended changes: _____

| Code | Project phase | Complete | Incomplete | Hours to date |
|------|---------------|----------|------------|---------------|
| 01 | Research | | | |
| 02 | Concept | | | |
| 03 | Layout | | | |
| 04 | Photography | | | |
| 05 | Copy/articles | | | |
| 06 | Scanning | | | |
| 07 | Art/illustrations | | | |
| 08 | Page layout | | | |
| 09 | Laser proofs | | | |
| 10 | Client approval | | | |
| 11 | Imagesetting | | | |
| 12 | Film proofs | | | |
| 13 | Client approval | | | |
| 14 | Printer | | | |
| 15 | Finishing operations | | | |
| 16 | Distribution | | | |
| | | | | |

Problems that could occur: _____

Contact us: ☐ Yes ☐ No

Desktop publisher: _____
Date: _____

## Headlines: 17/18 Dom Diagonal Bd BT

17 point type size on 18 points of leading

Space above 10 points, space below 12 points

Underline shifted down by 1.44 points

Left aligned

Hyphenation turned off

## Subhead: 14/15 Dom Diagonal BT Italic

*14 point type on 15 points of leading*

*Space above 6 points, space below 2 points*

*Left aligned*

*Hyphenation turned off*

Body Text: 11/13 Dutch801 Rm BT

11 point type on 13 points of leading

Space above 3 points

Justified on a line length of 27 picas

First line indent of 1 pica (except for the first paragraph of each section)

Samples: 10/12 FrnkGothITC Bk BT
10 point type on 12 points of leading
Space above 3.64 points
Left aligned
Rules are created with an underlined right aligned tab

AGREEMENT BETWEEN

_____

(name of photographer)
(hereinafter referred to as "the photographer")
— AND —

_____

(name of model)
(hereinafter referred to as "the model")

The parties agree as follows:

1. The model consents to and authorizes the use, by the photographer, and the photographer's respective representatives, licensees, successors, and assigns, of any photographs that the photographer has taken of the model and of the model's property, and of any reproductions of them, for any, including, but not limited to, the sale, publication, display, broadcast, and exhibition of them, in promotion, advertising, trade, and art, whether apart from or in connection with, or illustrative of, any other matter, without any further compensation to the model.

2. The model agrees that the photographs, reproductions, and negatives are the photographer's sole property, and that the photographer has the full right to dispose of any of them in any manner.

3. As the photographer proposes to act on this consent immediately, the model declares it to be irrevocable; and the model releases and discharges the photographer and his or her respective representatives, licensees, successors, and assigns, from all actions, causes of action, debts, accounts, contracts, claims, and demands which the model or the model's heirs, executors, administrators, or assigns have at any time as a result of any act or matter arising out of or in connection with the consent and authorization given by the model in this agreement.

IN WITNESS WHEREOF the parties to this agreement have executed this agreement.

**_If model is an adult:_**

(Signature of photographer) _____      (Signature of model)

Address and phone number of model          **_If model is a child:_**
or parent/guardian_____      I am the parent/guardian of the above-named model.

_____          I consent to the above on the model's behalf.

_____

_____

Date _____          (Signature of parent/guardian)

## Sample 16
## Cleaning up Electronic Files

You can use your computer to prepare files for our desktop publishing services. Please follow these guidelines when supplying computer-generated files so that we can produce your project within the time allotted and within the price estimate.

Some software programs can semi-automate this process. Make sure you make a copy of the file before you start.

### Extra formatting

- Convert or re-type uppercase headlines to upper and lowercase.
- Convert underlined text to italics.

### Special characters

- Convert double hyphens to em dashes or long dashes.
- Convert foot and inch marks to apostrophes and smart quotes.
- Add space before and after an en dash and ellipses (optional).
- Convert "I" to "1" and "O" to "0."
- Convert accents, bullets, copyright signs, fractions, and other characters.

### Extra characters

- Remove carriage returns within paragraphs.
- Remove carriage returns and tabs used to create hanging indents.
- Remove line feeds from ASCII text-only files.
- Remove spaces before punctuation marks including .,:;!?'"
- Remove spaces before and after tabs.
- Remove tabs used to indent first lines of body text (optional).
- Convert multiple spaces and tab stops to single tabs in tables.
- Replace double spaces with single spaces.
- Remove leading and trailing spaces in paragraphs.
- Remove multiple carriage returns.

Company: _____ Project number: _____

Project name/description: _____

✓      Place a check mark next to items that are proofed and approved.

X      Use an "x" to indicate items that are missing or incorrect.

N/A      Use "N/A" for items that don't apply to this proof.

| *Laser/fax proof*    *✓ or X or N/A* | *Blueline/color proofs*    *✓ or X or N/A* |
|---|---|
| Page content _____ | Trim _____ |
| Numbers _____ | Fold _____ |
| Headlines/subheads _____ | Diecut/perforate/punch _____ |
| Captions/quotes _____ | Halftones in position _____ |
| Color _____ | Reverses _____ |
| Call outs _____ | Registration _____ |
| Graphic treatments _____ | Proofed _____ |
| Type proofed _____ | Type/rules/graphics _____ |
| Phone numbers _____ | Halftones/screens _____ |
| Logos _____ | Color quality _____ |
| Layout/design _____ | Overprints/knockouts _____ |
| Crop/fold marks _____ | _____ |
| Halftones: cropped, sized ____ | _____ |
| Screens _____ | _____ |
| Postal indicia/codes/permits ___ | _____ |

Special notes or instructions _____

_____

This is to verify that I, the above-named client, representing the above-named company, have thoroughly reviewed and approved the project materials. I understand this is my last opportunity to request changes due to mistakes or preferences. I further acknowledge that any mistakes or preference changes that were not discovered or specified at this time are my responsibility, and not the designer/design company named above. I authorize the final phase of the project — the printed pieces.

Client signature: _____ Date: _____

## Sample 18
## Printing Instructions

**YOUR LOGO HERE**

Designer _____  Date _____

If questions, call _____

Project number _____  Project description _____

_____

Printer _____

Contact _____  Telephone _____

Materials sent _____

_____

### Printing specifications

Quantity _____  Number of sides _____

Print size _____  Finished size _____

Paper color _____  Paper stock _____

No. of colors _____  PMS ink no. _____  Varnish _____

Bleeds _____  Screens _____  Reverses _____

Halftones _____  Film _____  Separations _____

Proofs/blueline _____  Overlay _____  Laminated _____

Bindery/Fold _____  Drill _____  Score _____

Die cut _____  Perforations _____  Emboss _____

Other _____

Pack _____  Mailing _____

Delivery instructions _____

_____

_____

Date due _____  Shipping costs _____

Billing _____

Other instructions _____

## Sample 19
## Project Billing Worksheet

Client _____ Project number _____

Project name/description_____

_____

| Work Description | Time | Cost/hour | Total time cost |
|---|---|---|---|
| Client meetings _____ |
| Research _____ |
| Concept development _____ |
| Organization _____ |
| Layout/design _____ |
| Art direction _____ |
| Illustration _____ |
| Type mark-up _____ |
| Production_____ |
| Consulting with suppliers _____ |
| Copywriting/editing_____ |
| Proofing_____ |
| Press approvals _____ |
| Account administration _____ |
| Other _____ |

_____

### Sub-contractor/supplier prices

| Service | Price | Mark-up | Client's price |
|---|---|---|---|
| Photography _____ |
| Typesetting _____ |
| Film/camera supplies_____ |
| Other _____ |

**Total project cost** _____

# THE STUDIO

869 Main Street E
Pleasantville, State 23456
Tel: (101) 233-4444 Fax: (101) 233-4445

**INVOICE**

Invoice No. 1716

Date    June 12, 200-

SOLD TO:

Jane Doe

The Client's Office

123 Any Street

Anytown, State 12345

Tel: (101) 433-1234

Fax: (101) 433-1233

DELIVER TO:

Jane Doe

The Client's Office

123 Any Street

Anytown, State 12345

Tel: (101) 433-1234

Fax: (101) 433-1233

| | |
|---|---|
| Typesetting and layout of summer 20— issue of newsletter | $300.00 |
| SUB-TOTAL | $300.00 |
| TAX | 21.00 |
| TOTAL | $321.00 |
| DEPOSIT | 0.00 |
| BALANCE DUE | $321.00 |

GST R12345678
The Studio retains copyright unless previously otherwise agreed to in writing.
Accounts due on receipt. Unpaid accounts subject to 2 percent service charge per month.

## CHAPTER 9
# MANAGING YOUR BUSINESS

*If you want to fly a kite, you have to run against the wind.*

— BARBARA A. FANSON

It is possible to make $50,000 to $100,000 a year as a desktop publisher if you have 20 to 30 hours of billable time per week.

Chapter 8 contains a step-by-step description of project procedures. Now, what do you do after completing a project and invoicing the client? What do you actually do to keep the business operating efficiently?

## Twenty-Five Hours of Unbillable Time per Week

Managing a business requires time — approximately 25 hours of unbillable time per week. Billable time is time that can be charged to a client. Unbillable time is the work you do to operate your business, but which can't be charged to a client. To have a profitable business, keep your billable hours up, your expenses down, and your unbillable hours to a minimum.

Unbillable time usually includes about 14 hours of computer time, including time spent obtaining information; ordering and installing software upgrades; archiving electronic files; and client housekeeping such as updating notes, time sheets, and learning new software and upgrades. Unbillable time also includes any unbillable work on client jobs. For example, when you're starting out, it may take you twice as long to complete a project, so you might not bill the client for the entire time.

Unbillable time also includes about 11 hours of administrative time, including client contact, preparing quotations, unbillable meetings such as meetings with other desktop publishers or a networking meeting, recording work progress, tracking profit margins, invoicing, consultations with accountants or lawyers, talking to printers or service bureaus, and interviewing freelancers or employees.

By reducing some of the unbillable time, you'll have more time to work on client projects, or have more free time for yourself! Avoid making trips or paying for delivery to pick up supplies such as office supplies or printing. The printer could arrange delivery. Rather than going to pick up supplies, send a courier. A courier may charge less per hour than you.

Try to maintain existing clients. It takes more time and money to find a new client than to keep an existing one. More importantly, if you have the same clients repeatedly, you'll know how they pay and you won't need to fill out as many forms. For example, if you produce a newsletter for a client on a regular basis, you won't need to complete the client information form, the agreement, or establish style sheets every time you work on that client's projects. You'll reduce your unbillable time because you've reduced the amount of paperwork.

## Bookkeeping

Every business must keep accurate and thorough financial records covering all income received and expenses incurred. Records help you produce income, control expenses, plan growth and cash flow, keep tax payments to a minimum, and comply with the multitude of regulatory requirements.

Month:

| Date | Company | Sub-total | Sales tax (7%) | Balance |
|------|---------|-----------|----------------|---------|
| Jan. 9 | The Product Company | $100.00 | $7.00 | $107.00 |
| Jan. 11 | ABC Company | 200.00 | 14.00 | 214.00 |
| Jan. 12 | Sterling Communications | 300.00 | 21.00 | 321.00 |
| Jan. 15 | A Government Office | 500.00 | 35.00 | 535.00 |
| | *Total* | **$1,100.00** | **$77.00** | **$1,177.00** |

*Note:* Canadian residents should also account for any GST charged.

## Sample 22
## Cash Disbursements

Month:

| Number | Date | Payee | Amount | Sales tax | Supplies | Printing | Equipment | Draw |
|--------|------|-------|--------|-----------|----------|----------|-----------|------|
| 100 | Jan. 5 | The Office Place | $107.00 | $ 7.00 | $100.00 | | | |
| 101 | Jan. 6 | ABC Computers | 214.00 | 14.00 | | | $200.00 | |
| 102 | Jan. 7 | Me, The President | 500.00 | | | | | $500.00 |
| 103 | Jan. 8 | The Printing Place | 642.00 | 42.00 | | $600.00 | | |
| 104 | Jan. 9 | The Printing Place | 230.00 | 14.00 | | 216.00 | | |
| | | Total | $1,693.00 | $77.00 | $100.00 | $816.00 | $200.00 | $500.00 |

**Note:** *Canadian residents should also account for any* GST *charged.*

### An accountant or bookkeeper

When establishing a new business, you may wish to hire an accountant to design a system for recording the information for your own particular circumstance. A part-time bookkeeper could look after your books on a monthly basis for a lower hourly rate than an accountant.

If you prepare the invoice with an accounting software program, your income statement and related journals are automatically updated. Other businesses use a spreadsheet program to manually record invoices in a sales journal. Other businesses use a columnar book to manually write in journal entries.

Whichever method you choose to record sales and expenses, you should prepare an income statement monthly to check whether your total sales are more than your total expenses. You should review it to find how it can be improved next time around.

### Double-entry accounting

Double-entry accounting is the traditional method for keeping business records. Transactions are recorded into a journal, then monthly totals of those transactions are posted to the appropriate ledger accounts. Five categories of ledger accounts are income, expense, asset, liability, and net worth.

### Single-entry accounting

The single-entry accounting method is not as complete as a double-entry method, but it is relatively simple and records the flow of income and expenses through a daily summary of cash receipts, a monthly summary of receipts, and a monthly disbursements journal, such as a checkbook.

### Journals

Journals are formalized basic records for recording evidence of business transactions such as sales slips, invoices, checks, etc.

### Sales journal

A sales journal is a record of cash and charge sales. You will want to record your invoices in the sales journal either weekly or monthly. Record the gross amount, the sales tax charged, and net sales. Sample 21 is an example of a sales journal used to record the date, invoice number, company name, sub-total, sales taxes, and net balance of a job. By recording all your sales on a spreadsheet, you can quickly calculate taxes to remit and totals.

### Cash receipts and disbursements journal

A cash disbursements journal records all cash outlays for purchases, expenses, payroll, cash withdrawals, and loan payments. A cash receipts journal records all cash sales, bank deposits, and receipts on account from a client. The two journals should help you maintain your current bank balance. If you take your bank balance after doing a bank reconciliation report, add the total from the cash receipts journal, and subtract the total from the cash payments journal, the total will be how much money your business currently has in the bank. Sample 22 is an example of a cash disbursements journal used to record checks, the date, and which type of expense occurred.

### Expenses journal

Weekly or monthly, you may want to record all your expenses: cash receipts and check stubs. If you paid for the art supplies out of your pocket, that represents a capital investment by the owner.

### Synoptic journal

The most common and easiest journal to keep is a synoptic journal, or a combined journal with a separate column for each major account. Everything is recorded on one journal: cash receipts, cash payments, sales, expenses, and, perhaps, accounts receivable and accounts payable.

### Ways to record bookkeeping entries

If you prepare the invoice with an accounting software program, your income statement and related journals are automatically updated. My bookkeeper comes twice a month and uses Multiledger on my computer to keep track of how much money I have in the bank, calculate sales tax remittances, and keep track of income and expenses. AccPac Simply Accounting, Quicken, and MYOB (Mind Your Own Business) are other accounting software programs available.

Some businesses use a spreadsheet program to manually record invoices in a sales journal. Other businesses use a columnar book to manually write in journal entries.

A balance sheet reveals your financial position at a particular moment in time.

Whichever method you choose to record sales and expenses, you should prepare an income statement monthly to check whether your total sales are more than your total expenses. You should review it to find how it can be improved next month.

A balance sheet is a listing of assets, liabilities, and capital. Assets–liabilities=capital. Assets are things of value that the business has, such as a bank account, accounts receivable, and investments. Liabilities are money that is owed, such as bank loans and accounts payable. Your assets should be greater than your liabilities. Accounts receivable is money owed to you by clients. Your accounts receivables should be less than 90 days old. Accounts payable is the money you owe suppliers or others who have extended credit to your business. Try to pay your bills promptly to avoid penalties or interest charges.

## Recording entries

Whenever I receive an invoice, it is placed in the Unposted Accounts Payable file folder. When my bookkeeper comes twice a month, she records these invoices in Multiledger. After the invoices are posted, they are placed in the Posted Accounts Payable folder. When I write a check to pay an invoice, I scribble the check number and the date paid on the invoice. The paid invoice is filed alphabetically in file folders. Usually a company check will have a stub to record information for your records. Be sure to write the check amount and the tax amount on your stub or copy as a method of double-checking.

## Financial records

### Profit and loss statement

Once a month, you should total your sales, subtract your expenses, and determine whether your business made a profit or loss. If your sales are greater than your expenses, obviously you made a profit.

### Balance sheet

A balance sheet reveals your financial position at a particular moment in time. To determine your financial position, you will need to know your assets, liabilities, and owner's equity.

### Assets

Assets are anything of worth to the business including: properties, money, accounts receivable, merchandise, inventory, supplies, equipment, and buildings. Current assets can be converted to cash within a short period of time. Fixed assets, such as land, are not cashed in at just any time.

### Liabilities

Liabilities are your business debts including: accounts payable (debts), loans, and mortgages. Current liabilities, such as accounts payable, will be paid off in a short period of time, whereas long term liabilities, such as mortgage or lease agreements, may take several years to pay off.

### Owner's Equity

Owner's Equity is the difference between your assets and liabilities. The owner's equity should equal the amount of net income or loss on the year end income statement plus the owner's investment less any withdrawals for the year.

## Taxation and Your Business

As tax laws are different from country to country, be sure to check with your local office to find out about regulations that will affect you. As a general rule, save all business-related receipts even before you start a business. When you do start, you can claim business-related expenses incurred in the last two or three years.

Every year, you will have to submit financial information to the government to see if you have to pay taxes on the income you earned. If your business is registered as a sole proprietorship, you'll file the annual income tax form whereby any tax breaks you have will be subtracted from the income you made from your business and other sources. According to a formula, you will find out if you owe the government money, or whether you'll get a refund.

If you have an incorporated business, you'll have to prepare financial statements and submit them to the government.

The trick is to reduce the amount of income tax you'll have to pay to the government. Here are six strategies that you can consider:

Car expenses can be claimed proportionate to the amount of business use.

### Sell your equipment

Many people have a desk, filing cabinet, calculator, or other business furniture and equipment before they start a business. Since the equipment has a value, sell it to your business. That value increases the amount of investment you make to your business, thereby decreasing your taxable income.

### Claims for home-based businesses

If you do some or all of your work at home, you can claim a portion of your household expenses when calculating your business expenses. Household insurance, mortgage interest, property tax, utilities (including telephone, gas, or hydro), and maintenance costs can be considered expenses to operating a business. Most accountants would advise a business to claim one-sixth of household expenses if one-sixth of the home is used for work-related activities.

### Claim vehicle expenses

If your vehicle is used for business, a portion of the car maintenance can also be claimed. Car insurance, maintenance, payments, and gas can be claimed proportionately. Like household costs, the amount of car expenses that can be claimed are proportional to the amount of business use. If the vehicle is used for business two-thirds of the time, and one-third for pleasure, you can claim two-thirds of the operating costs.

### Travel expenses

Did you know that your next trip could be considered a business expense if you perform a business-related activity while there? Travel costs can be declared if you research suppliers or equipment, attend a seminar or trade show, negotiate with dealers or clients, attend an association meeting, or potentially increase your business's revenue. Plan at least one activity each day — even just one hour — so you can claim the expense.

### Education

Every time you take a class, attend a trade show, or subscribe to industry magazines, you can claim it as a necessary expense for improving your business. You can also claim parking receipts for attending a class or trade show.

### Meals and promotion

Claim 50 percent of meals and entertainment expenses if you operate a service business, because anyone is a potential client. Record the date, names, and reason on the back of the receipt (in case you're audited).

## Business Forms

Business forms should be efficient, professional looking, and reduce payment delays. Each business form has a function, so design them so they're easy to fill in.

Chapter 8 discusses designing an invoice in detail.

## Credit Card Merchant Status

You can become a Visa or MasterCard merchant by filling out an application at the bank. Most banks do not charge for the application, but they do keep a percentage of the deposit. At the time this book was written Visa's rate was 4.5 percent while MasterCard's rate was 3.55 percent. For example, if a client pays $300 with his or her Visa, the bank will keep $13.50 and deposit the remainder into the your bank account. You may also be required to pay about $1 per month for the use of an imprinter (the machine that make an impression of the credit card onto the receipt).

Although I can accept payments by Visa or MasterCard, I have had only one client who pays by credit card. Most companies prefer to pay by company check.

## Collection Tips for Accounts

Most experts agree that maintaining a proper cash flow is one of the most important factors in operating a successful business.

### Minimizing the risk

Some cash flow problems arise when your customers accounts continue to go unpaid. Statistics show that the longer an account goes unpaid, the greater the risk that it will not be paid in full. Unless you are paid in advance, you always run a risk of not being paid. But the risk can be minimized by taking a few precautions:

- Get to know your customer.

- Make sure the terms of payment are clearly understood.
- Bill promptly.
- Keep dated accounts receivable records.
- Do a follow up on payments that are outstanding.

Also, if you are a member, contact the credit bureau to request a credit history on your customer; the information may be useful in helping make a decision to extend credit.

I often ask new clients for a deposit up front, especially if printing or other outside expenses are involved. If newsletters are being stuffed into envelopes and mailed by an outside direct mail house, the mail house usually wants the postage to be paid before the newsletters are actually mailed. Why should your money be tied up? Ask the client for a certain amount and the balance on delivery.

### Collecting outstanding accounts

Regardless of all the steps you have taken, some accounts will still be delinquent. After implementing the standard collections procedure, your next step is to try collecting the account by telephone or by letter, starting with gentle reminders and increasing to a firm demand for payment. Sample 23 is an example of a letter to collect an outstanding account.

If collection letters don't work, you will need to decide whether to take further action, such as referring the account to a paralegal, credit agency, or lawyer. How much you're willing to pay for collection and how large the amount of the outstanding bill is, are going to be factors in determining who you decide to hire.

### Small Claims Court

If a civil court action has to be filed as the final step to collect the account, check what the limit for your area is. For example, the limit is $6,000 for the Toronto area (exclusive of interest and costs).

Since some businesses cannot afford the time, or do not have the experience to deal with the court system, an expert who specializes in Small Claims litigation may be helpful in collecting outstanding accounts.

January 20, 200-

R.U. Sleeping
ABC Waterbed Company
123 Any Street
Anytown, State, 16532

Dear Mr. Sleeping:

I have looked everywhere and I can't find it. I have looked in my filing cabinet, in the trash can, under the desk, and I still can't find it. I was looking for your payment of invoice no. 123 for $500.

If you happen to find a check with our name on it, could you please mail it to us.

Meanwhile, I'll keep looking.

Yours truly,

Your company name

Barbara A. Fanson

President

# WORKING EFFICIENTLY

*We are lead to believe that if you work hard, you'll get ahead.*

*If you work hard and smart, you'll go further, faster.*

— BARBARA A. FANSON

Working on a project is similar to doing a puzzle. The pieces are laid out and you have a picture of what it should look like in the end. As you assemble the pieces one by one in logical order, you can see how the pieces are connected. Every piece is vital to completing the picture.

Tackling a project is much the same. With a mental picture of what the final artwork should look like, you organize the steps you need to take in a logical sequence. Once the steps are organized, you can easily move through each stage of the project.

Planning does pay. One minute of planning can save four minutes of spinning your tires. For every hour you spend planning, you can knock off about four hours of wasted time. If you complete a project in less time, you can handle more projects, and bring in more money.

If you work smarter and more efficiently, you'll be more profitable. If you establish a routine for doing the unbillable paperwork, then you'll have more time to devote to billable projects.

Chapter 8 dealt with the step-by-step procedures needed to do a project. This Chapter will deal, in detail, with how to do desktop publishing more efficiently. If you find that you are familiar with some of the step by step instructions, feel free to skip over to the next section.

Invest in computer training.

## Increase the Amount of Time You Spend on a Project

The more time you spend on a project, the more profitable you'll become. For example, compare a one-page flyer to an eight-page newsletter. Both projects require about the same amount of unbillable hours: time spent on client consultation, preparing job dockets, recording expenses, tracking time spent, dealing with printers, preparing an invoice, and archiving the file. Let's say the one-page flyer requires one hour of billable time to complete, while the eight-page newsletter requires at least eight hours of billable time to complete. For each one-hour flyer you prepare, you will likely do almost as much unbillable work as you do for the eight-hour newsletter. Since you would need to prepare eight flyers to make what you would on the newsletter, you will be doing eight times the amount of unbillable work! Make sure your unbillable time is less than your billable time.

## Learn the Software Thoroughly

Increase your efficiency by using your software's features of style sheets, master pages, and paragraph formatting when you produce publications, sales literature, and business forms in a page layout program.

I charge $60 per page to produce black-and-white publications. I used to allow myself about one hour per page. When I became more adept with the software, I was able to typeset and lay out a page in 20 minutes. And I'm still charging $60 per page! I'm still making $240 for a four-page newsletter, but I'm doing it in less than two hours. By developing shortcuts, I can do the work in less time, but at the same per-page rate.

The first time I work on a project, it takes a little longer to design it. Typefaces and sizes have to be chosen, the grid has to be established, and I create style sheets and master pages in a page layout program on the computer. The second time I do the project, I can open up the old document, save it with another name, delete the text, and typeset the new text.

To become a profitable desktop publisher, you will have to know essential software programs and develop an understanding of the graphics industry. Invest in computer training.

Determine your best way of learning a software program. Is it attending instructor-led classes, reading step-by-step tutorial books, watching videotapes, or listening to audiotapes?

Discuss your training objectives with private and public training institutions and find out what courses they offer. Do you want day, evening, or weekend classes? Are you willing to travel?

If you are considering instructor-led classes, ask about the instructor's background. You don't want an instructor who just knows the program: you will probably want an instructor who uses the program regularly to create projects. Has the instructor produced four-color projects that require a knowledge of trapping and color separations? Will the trainer provide a course manual so you don't have to take as many notes in class? Will there be an opportunity to practice the software?

## Create Style Sheets

### What are style sheets?

Style sheets in a page layout or word processing program are used to store information about the type size, font, and style of headlines, body text, cutlines, etc., in a particular file. If you set up style sheets, you will become more efficient, maintain consistency, and you will be able to make changes to the layout much faster. Even Web page design programs such as Macromedia Dreamweaver have style sheets to maintain consistency among Web pages and increase efficiency.

When you decide which typeface and size you are going to use for headlines, save that style. You'll then be able to change, for example, from 24-point Helvetica bold headlines to 10-point Times body text instantly. Creating style sheets also maintains consistency — all your headlines will be the same: 24-point

Helvetica bold. But most importantly, it's easier to change a style sheet than to change every headline in your document. If you decide to change the size or font of your headlines after the project has been completed, you can just change the style for headlines; all the headlines based on that style sheet will automatically change.

Style sheets are usually saved with the document, but some software programs let you pick up styles from a previous document. Or, if you open the previous document, save it with a new name, the style sheets are already available.

## Creating style sheets

### Microsoft Word

You can create a style by choosing Style from the Format menu. Or, you can use a style that MS Word has supplied from the Style dialog box. You can assign a keyboard shortcut to your style sheet in the Style dialog box. You can also change from one style to another by clicking on the style pop-up menu on the formatting tool bar above your document.

### QuarkXPress

QuarkXPress does not supply any preformatted style sheets, so you'll have to create them. To create a style sheet in QuarkXPress, choose Style Sheets from the Edit menu. After creating style sheets in QuarkXPress, there are four ways to apply them. If you have an extended keyboard with function keys across the top, you can program the function keys with different style sheets. For example, F5 could give you headlines. You can also program the keypad so that pressing a number on the keypad will give you a certain style. Or, you can choose a style sheet from the Style Sheet palette or choose Style Sheets from the Style menu.

### Adobe PageMaker

If you are using Adobe PageMaker, you can use a style sheet that is supplied with the page layout program, or you can create your own. To edit or create a style sheet, choose Define Styles from the Type menu. A dialog box will appear. Choose Body text from the list of style sheets on the left and click on the Edit button to alter the style. A second dialog box will appear, allowing you to change the type specifications, paragraph formatting, tabs, or hyphenation. Unfortunately, you cannot assign a keyboard shortcut, function key, or keypad shortcut to your style sheets in PageMaker. To change from one style sheet to another, click on one in the Styles palette or choose Style from the Type menu.

I find the style sheets that come with PageMaker to be limited, especially when compared to QuarkXPress. For example, if I want to create a style with a drop cap for the first paragraph of each story of a newsletter, I cannot access drop caps from within the Styles dialog box. Also, PageMaker won't let me save a style with mixed type sizes, as QuarkXPress will. I find I am slightly less productive when using PageMaker instead of QuarkXPress.

### Adding hyphenation to style sheets

Most page layout and word processing programs will allow you to alter the hyphenation defaults for that program. But, did you know you can change the hyphenation for individual style sheets?

When typesetting headlines or promotional copy, you may want to turn off auto hyphenation, so there are no hyphens. But, you may want to keep hyphenation on for body text. You can have different kinds of hyphenation in the same document if you set up style sheets and change the hyphenation values.

#### Hyphenation in MS Word

To turn automatic hyphenation on or off in Microsoft Word, choose Paragraph from the Format menu. Make sure the Text Flow options are showing. Check the box "Don't Hyphenate."

To create a new style sheet, choose Style from the Format menu. A dialog box will appear. Click on the New button; the New Style dialog box will appear. Name the style Headline. Click on the Format button and choose Paragraph from the pop-up menu. If you click in the Don't Hyphenate check box, an "x" will appear, and your headlines won't hyphenate.

When creating a style sheet for body text, if you don't want hyphenation, make sure the Don't Hyphenate box is checked.

#### Hyphenation in QuarkXPress

In QuarkXPress, choose H&Js (Hyphenation and Justification) from the Style menu. The standard hyphenation in QuarkXPress is auto hyphenation. Click on the Edit button of the Standard hyphenation style and another dialog box appears. You can turn auto hyphenation on or off. Or, you can create a new hyphenation style and use it with your headline style sheet.

You could set up a style sheet for headlines with auto hyphenation turned off and another style sheet for body text with auto hyphenation turned on.

To create a style sheet for headlines in QuarkXPress, choose Style Sheets from the Edit menu. A dialog box appears. Click the New button and another dialog box appears. Name this style Headline and click on the Format button. Change H&Js from Standard to your hyphenation style.

To create a style sheet for body text with auto hyphenation turned on, choose Style Sheets from the Edit menu. A dialog box appears. Click the New button and another dialog box appears. Name this style Body Text and click on the Format button. Change H&Js to Standard.

### Adobe PageMaker

To turn hyphenation on or off in PageMaker, choose Hyphenation from the Type menu. A dialog box appears where you can make the change. With auto hyphenation, PageMaker will also hyphenate capitalized words, including city names.

Version 6.5 does not allow you to create more than one hyphenation style. For example, when producing promotional literature and publications, you may want hyphenation turned off for headlines but turned on for body text. If hyphenation is turned on, you will need to select one story or headline and change the hyphenation to off; keep hyphenation turned on for the rest.

## Create Headers and Footers in Microsoft Word

If you are using Microsoft Word, you have the option of creating headers and footers. A header appears at the top of every page. A footer appears at the bottom of every page. Headers and footers can be text, automatic page numbers, the title of your document, or a graphic element such as rules, boxes, logos, or art.

To create a header or footer in Microsoft Word, choose Header and Footer from the View menu. By setting up a header or footer, you need to typeset or lay it out only once, and all the pages will be consistent.

You can adjust headers and footers so they don't show up on the first page, or change their position on the page by increasing the amount of space from the edge of the paper. You can also set up mirrored headers and footers, so that an automatic page number appears on the outside edge of your left-hand and right-hand pages.

## Create Master Pages

In page layout programs such as QuarkXPress and Adobe PageMaker, there is no header and footer option. Instead you need to set up a master page. Anything you put on the master page will show up on all your pages that are based on that master page. You could add rules, text, boxes, and an automatic page number to the master page and it will print out on all the pages based on that master page.

Every document comes with one master page, but you could create other master pages to have different layouts throughout your publication. For example, master A could have three columns. Any page based on master A would have three columns. If you are going to use master B for classified advertisements, you might want four columns, instead of three. Any page based on master B would have four columns.

Master pages in QuarkXPress are more flexible than PageMaker. If you put something on a master page in Quark, it can be deleted, moved, or altered on different pages in your publication. If you put something on the master page in PageMaker, you can either view all the master page items or turn them all off. You cannot delete one item from a page, if it was placed on the master page. Instead, you have to draw a rectangle over it to hide it.

What should you include on a master page? If there is anything that appears on every page such as a rule, box, screen, or type, you can create it once on the master page and it will show up on every page that is based on that master page. Usually, layout artists include identifying text such as automatic page numbers, name of publication, issue date, or a copyright notice. If there's a photo or graphic on every page, position it once on the master page.

Automatic page numbers must be set up on the master page in QuarkXPress and PageMaker. In Quark, press the Command + 3 keys; in PageMaker, press the Command + Option + P keys. This will automatically number your pages so that page one will read 1, page two will read 2, and so on. You can also change the starting page number by choosing Section from the Page menu in Quark, and choose Document Setup from the File menu in PageMaker.

I can be more efficient using QuarkXPress to create a publication than Adobe PageMaker, because the program is more flexible and has more time-saving functions than PageMaker. For example, I will probably have a headline across the top of every page of my publication. I can draw a text box across the top of the master page and it will show up on every page. I can type some text on the master page and change the size, font, and type style. This text will show up on every page — and it's editable! I can highlight that text on page four, delete it, and type something else. That can't be done in PageMaker. If you type something on the master page in PageMaker, it cannot be altered on other pages — either use it or hide it!

You can also click in the headline text box on the master page and format the flashing cursor. Change the font, type size, style, and color of the desired type. When you go to page three, just click in the headline text box and the cursor is already formatted to give you the desired size and font.

When laying out a publication in Quark, I can also draw text boxes for columns of body text and link them. I can also create irregular column widths such as two wide columns and a narrow one.

If you turned on Facing Pages when you created the new document, you would have a left master page and a right master page. Anything you put on the left master page will show up only on left-hand pages. So, I set up the left master page first, and then duplicate it for the right master page.

Some designers lay out page numbers on the outside edge of a page. For example, the page number would be on the left side of a left-hand page and on the right side of a right-hand page. To do this, you have to have Facing Pages activated when creating a new document.

## Clean up Client-Supplied Text Files

The basic rules of typing, such as capitals at the start of a sentence and breaks between paragraphs, apply to text inputting on a computer. However, desktop publishing brings some new rules to text formatting.

Sometimes when designing a page with a page layout application, if the copy has been supplied on a word processing diskette, it takes a long time to format and cancel all the extra commands that have been entered. It is sometimes easier to just re-enter the copy, rather than re-format the word processing. Here are some guidelines to avoid when word processing:

- When typing, allow the text to wrap off the right side of the screen; it will automatically come down to the next line. Only press the return/enter key between headings and paragraphs.

- Only one return between paragraphs is required if the text is to be brought into a page layout application. These programs have paragraph spacing to adjust the space between paragraphs. (You can format a paragraph so that when you press the return key additional space between paragraphs is added automatically.)

- Only one space after a period or colon is required. DTP applications work with proportional type spacing and therefore the space between words is regulated by the characters on that line. Two spaces after a period or colon produces ugly rivers of white space in blocks of text.

- Formatting is kept to a minimum if the text is to be brought into a page layout application. These programs handle the alignment, spacing, and attributes of text much more powerfully.

- Indents and hanging indents are handled with the ruler settings and should not be set with manual spaces or tabs.

While some of the powerful features found in page layout applications have made their way into these word processing applications, it is still better to format the text in an application designed to handle all type attributes and sizes with some built-in graphics capabilities.

## Change the Reader's Spreads to Printer's Spreads

Most page layout programs lay out pages in reader's spreads — the way readers would view them as they turn the pages. Your commercial print shop prefer printer's spreads. There are six ways to change reader's spreads to printer's spreads:

- **Let the printer worry about it.** Supply a diskette, paper, or film to the print shop and let the printer arrange your pages into printer's spreads.

- **Purchase a Quark Xtension called Printer's Spreads for US $179.** This extension — which is added to your version of QuarkXPress — will arrange your pages into printer's spreads.

- **Purchase a page imposition software program.** Programs such as Adobe PressWise and Impostrip will arrange QuarkXPress or PageMaker pages (and other PostScript files) into 2-up printers spreads, 4-up work-and-turn, or 8-up gang — whichever way you want. These programs sell for about $2,000.

- **Ask your service bureau or print shop if it has an imposition program.** It may have the software to output your file in printer's spreads.

- **Create tabloid (17" x 11") pages and manually lay out two letter-sized pages on each.** For example, if you were creating an eight-page publication, you would create four tabloid pages — each containing two pages.

- **Cheat! Manually move your pages into printer's spreads.** You can set up a brand new document and manually alter the page numbers or you can move the pages just before you output them. For example, if you were creating an eight-page publication, add a ninth page and make it your front page. So, whenever you want to work on your front page, you'll go to page 9. Leave the real page 1 blank. Change page 3 into page 7 and change page 7 into 3. When you send the file to the service bureau, make sure it outputs pages 2 to 9 only, because if it outputs your blank page 1, it'll charge you for it.

## Efficient Computer Files Output Quickly

If you take your completed QuarkXPress or Adobe PageMaker files to a service bureau to output, you may pay extra if your files take longer to output.

Some desktop publishers take their computer files to a service bureau because the bureau can output the files with more lines of resolution, producing a better-quality output on paper or film. The service bureau will charge $8 to $20 per page to output the file. It is assumed that each page will take about five minutes. If your job takes longer to output, the service bureau may charge up to $100 per hour.

Here are some tips for keeping your file size small and, therefore, outputting faster and easier:

### Crop photos in an image-editing program before importing them into a page layout program

You could import and crop (mask) a photo in a page layout program so that a portion of the photo does not show, and therefore, will not print. But the file size of the photo is still the same — whether you crop in a page layout program or not. To reduce the file size, open the photo in an image-editing program such as Adobe Photoshop. Use the cropping tool to select an area and crop the rest. The file size of the photo will be reduced, which will speed up your processing time.

### Rectangular photos will output faster than ovals, rounded corners, or polygons

With desktop publishing, you can have a photo with rounded corners or a photo inside an oval border. It is easy to alter the appearance of a photo, but a simple, rectangular shape will output the fastest.

To import a photo into QuarkXPress, you need to draw a picture box first. QuarkXPress has four picture box tools for you to choose from. The rectangular picture box will output faster than the other shapes. The irregular-shaped polygon will output the slowest.

---

**CREATIVE DESIGN TIPS TO SAVE YOU MONEY**

1. **Stick to your format.** Resist the temptation to change the number of columns, the width of columns, the placement of regular features, and typefaces.

2. **Avoid bleeds.** Photos or artwork that run off the page require extra paper, trimming, and therefore cost more to print.

3. **Avoid tight registration.** Duotones, color separations, and two colors placed very close to each other require extra care during the printing process and may increase your production costs.

4. **Scallop columns.** You can align all columns at the top and leave the bottom of the text scalloped (uneven). Scalloped columns let you concentrate on content, rather than precision layout.

5. **Use screen tints.** Use a different screen percentage of a single ink color to create a tint that gives you the effect of a second ink color. Overlapping screens of two different colors can create a third or fourth color.

6. **Design your publication for self-mailing.** Save the cost of envelopes, stuffing, and sealing by creating a mailing panel on the back page of a publication.

---

### Avoid rotating photos or text, since they require more processing time

It is easy to rotate a photo or text in a page layout or word processing program, but it will not output as fast as an item that has not been rotated.

### Change color photos and artwork to grayscale if you're not printing them in color

Color photos have a larger file size than grayscale, so if you're not producing a four-color publication, change it. You can open a color photo in Adobe Photoshop, for example, and change the mode to grayscale.

### Black-and-white screen captures have a smaller file size than color screen captures

If you are creating a screen capture to demonstrate something on the computer screen, change your color monitor to black and white. If you are printing the screen capture with black ink, you don't need a larger, color screen capture.

## Keep in Style

Use the real version of a font. For example, use Bookman Italic rather than changing the style to Italic. When fonts are designed, there are different kerning values for Bookman and Bookman Italic. If you use the font, but changed the style to Italic, some fonts will not output it with Italic. An imagesetter may output the actual font you used.

To ensure that QuarkXPress uses the real font, for example, Bookman Italic, rather than changing the style of plain old Bookman to Italic, use the Font Usage dialog box in the Utilities menu. This box will detect the imposters and you can replace them.

   (a)  Search for the font you have selected. If you see something in brackets — other than <Plain>, follow step b.

   (b)  Replace it with the true Italic version of the font. Make sure that, in addition to specifying your font in the box, the "Plain" box is checked under style.

Always use the real version of a font.

## Change Color of Trim Marks

Let's assume you've created a business card with two colors of ink — black and magenta. If you draw your own trim marks on the corners of the card, you would use the Line Tool to draw the trim marks. You could print color separations so that everything that is black comes out on one sheet of paper, and everything that is magenta on another. Your black trim marks would come out on the black piece of paper only. There would be no trim marks on the magenta piece of paper. Change the color of the trim marks to registration, and they should print out on every sheet of paper when you output color separations.

If there are any items that you want to print out on every sheet of your color separations, change the color to registration.

## Working with Photo CDs

Scanned color photos require a lot of memory (two megabytes or more), so you can't save them on diskettes. You have to invest in an external storage device, such as a Zip drive. CD-ROMs (Compact Disk - Read Only Memory) are another method of storing large files.

You can take a regular roll of 35mm film to a color film lab and have it scanned onto a Photo CD. The film lab will charge about $5 to process a roll of film, $20 for the Photo CD, and $1 for each photograph to be scanned and saved on the Photo CD. A Photo CD will hold about 100 photographs so you can add more photographs later.

You can import a photo from a CD-ROM into a page layout program for previewing, but there are a few steps to take before you can output color separations.

(a) Open up the photo in an image-editing program such as Adobe Photoshop or Adobe Photostyler. Is the scan sharp, or do you need to apply a sharpening filter? Do you need to do some color retouching?

(b) Change the mode to grayscale (for black and white) or CMYK (cyan, magenta, yellow, and black for process color).

(c) Change the resolution of your image. Photos are scanned with a resolution of 72 pixels per inch (ppi). You'll want to change the image resolution to about twice your desired line screen. For example, if you want a halftone line screen of 150 dpi, change the resolution to 300 ppi.

(d) Save your file with a file format such as EPS or TIFF.

# 22 COST CUTTING TIPS

- Fewer pages, fewer copies, or fewer issues per year will reduce costs. Consult with your client.

- Use standard paper sizes, colors, and weights.

- Obtain estimates from several designers, typesetters, printers, and paper suppliers.

- Planning will help you develop a schedule and define your needs.

- Be informed by learning about computer graphics, scanners with optical character recognition, word processors, and web presses.

- If you know another publisher, perhaps you can pool supplies and services.

- Buy paper in quantity.

- If you have the same spot color for every issue, you can have it printed in advance and stored at the print shop. (For example, if you preprint a year's supply of a blue nameplate for a publication, then you will just have to print the black ink for each issue.)

- Obtain a contract for services over long periods. A printer may give you a better rate if you commit yourself for a year.

- Use lighter-weight paper.

- Ask your printer if he or she has any paper in storage that can be used. Ask for a good rate. The printer may have a stock paper or house paper that is ordered in bulk quantities.

- Take your own photographs. With a photography class, you may develop your own photos.

- Use photocopiers with enlargement and reduction features instead of photostats. A stat will cost at least $5, whereas a photocopy may be 25 cents.

- Gang photographs. If all your photographs are being halftoned the same size, they can be shot at the same time.

- Avoid bleeds, tight registrations, and other specialty printing orders.

By printing two similar projects on larger paper, you can save money.

- Every change or correction costs money, so proofread every document before hiring a typesetter.
- Don't pay for any artwork or printing that is inferior. If it is not what you asked for, have it re-done.
- If a supplier offers a discount for prompt payment, take advantage of it.
- Deliver work on time to avoid overtime charges. Enforce deadlines because delays cost money.
- Talk to other desktop publishers or printers. Perhaps they can suggest ways to reduce costs or publish more efficiently.
- If you are producing a newsletter, always think in groups of four, since most standard newsletters are printed on 17" x 11" paper and folded to create four pages. If you have more than four pages, keep page counts in multiples of four.
- Make sure your typesetter has memory so that minor changes can be easily accommodated.

## Proofread

Proofread the document. Errors caught at this stage in the production cycle will cost you a lot less than those caught later, once the document is at the printer. Review the discussion on proofreading in Chapter 8.

## Output Two Files on One Larger Sheet of Film

If you have two assignments that need to be output by a service bureau onto film with similar film specifications, you could save money by outputting both of them onto one larger sheet of film, reducing your expenses. For example, most service bureaus have a minimum size of 8 ½" x 11" and charge at least $8 for letter-sized paper. A tabloid sheet 17" x 11" is about $12 to output. If two projects will fit onto letter- or legal-sized film, output them together: you will save money by outputting the two smaller pages onto one larger one.

## Gang Two Jobs Together for Printing

If you have two similar projects that both have to be printed with the same ink and paper specifications, consider ganging them together to save money. By printing two similar projects on larger paper, you could save money since less printing plates and film are required. You may also save on set-up time.

## Communicate with Your Print Shop

Make sure you talk to your printer and other suppliers before beginning any assignment. Will your printer be printing one business card or four-up butting? Never assume. Ask your printer before you start. One time, I supplied artwork for one business card. The print shop wanted to print four-up, so they made three stats of my art so they would have four pieces of art and charged me for the three stats! If I had asked the printer how he wanted the art supplied I could have saved money by supplying four pieces of art, rather than one. See Chapter 11, Dealing with Suppliers, for more about communicating with your printer.

## Update Hardware and Software

As a desktop publisher, you are relying on your computer equipment to operate efficiently and to output your projects quickly. You will want to upgrade your computer from time to time by adding more RAM memory or hard disk memory. As your skills progress and you get faster, you may want to get a faster computer.

Most software programs are updated annually to add more capabilities to the program or to get rid of minor quirks or conflicts with other utilities. Some upgrades offer more automated tasks that enable you to be more efficient. If you plan to have your electronic files output by a service bureau, you will have to upgrade your software so you will be compatible.

To keep your computer equipment and software running at optimum speed, purchase the upgrades. They are usually worth it.

CHAPTER **11**

# DEALING WITH SUPPLIERS

*Hard work, honesty, and discipline are the keys to success.*

*With them, you can open any door.*

— NINA COCO

If you are running a desktop publishing business, you'll need to deal with suppliers, including printers, service bureaus, and contractors such as writers, editors, illustrators, photographers, and other desktop publishers.

It is important that you establish a good working relationship from the beginning. What do you expect from them? What are their expectations of you? How soon will they be paid? Are discounts available? How should the artwork be supplied?

## Dealing with Print Shops

A good print shop is not determined by price alone. A good printer is someone you can work with to produce a successful printed piece that's accurate and delivered on time. The relationship between the print shop's production manager and the printer is very important.

## Choosing a print shop

Printing shops vary in the quality of their work, the services offered, and the prices charged. Some printers do two-color printing, which usually means black ink plus one spot color. Others specialize in four-color printing. Some printers have a variety of bindery and finishing equipment to complete the work. Other printers farm out binding. Some printers specialize in business stationery or business forms or books.

Obtain at least three quotations for the printing of your project. Sample 9 is an example of a printing bid request which can be faxed to printers with specific information for preparing a quote.

Obtain quotes from several printers and don't get too comfortable with one printer. Compare prices and look for quality. You may get a better price outside the city, but if it's a two-hour drive, you may not be saving money. Ask to see samples of the printer's recent work. Does it look professional? Is the printing clear? Are there messy ink spots, hickeys, smudges, or tears in the paper?

If you plan to print a regular publication, you can save money by purchasing paper in bulk and storing it at the print shop. Avoid buying paper in bulk until you know the project will be ongoing.

Before starting a project, discuss it with your printer. How much will it cost? How long will it take to print and finish?

## Supplying artwork

Before starting a project, you should ask your printer several questions about the artwork. If you're preparing an advertisement to be printed in a newspaper or magazine, call the publication and speak to the production manager to find out the following details.

(a) How should the artwork be supplied? On diskette, paper, or film?

(b) Should you supply negative film or positive film?

(c) Should negative film be right-reading, emulsion up or down?

(d) What line screen will be used on halftones?

Obtain at least three quotations for the printing of your project.

(e) How should you lay out the project — in printer's spreads, reader's spreads, two-up, or four-up?

(f) If it is a four-color printing job, what kind of color proofs should you supply?

(g) What is the deadline for submitting the artwork to get the project printed on time?

Sample 18 is a printing instruction sheet you can use to record particulars about your project when submitting it to a printer.

## Communicating with your print shop

Here are some tips to facilitate your relationship with your printer.

- Keep a file of printed samples that represent the kind of printing you want, and discuss them with your printer.

- Some print shops specialize in certain items and sub-contract out work they cannot handle. Keep track of who does what well. (I use four printers regularly: one for web printing, one for instant printing, one for fine color jobs, and one for thermo-engraved business stationery.)

- Supply a sample dummy with your camera-ready art to show how it will be folded. It may also be a stock sample.

- Ask your printer for cost-saving ideas.

- Communicate with your printer. As soon as something goes wrong or there is a delay in the project, let your printer know.

- When placing an order, confirm the proofing and delivery dates.

- Stay in touch with your printer or representative during the printing process.

- Pay attention to reprint costs.

- All good relationships are based on mutual give and take, so be flexible.

- During uncertain economic times, print shops can go under almost overnight. Make sure your artwork isn't inside when the locks are changed. Watch for signs of instability.

## MONEY SAVING PRINTING TIPS

- It is possible to print appealing, effective pieces without spending a lot of money. Keep your design simple and straightforward, and produce it carefully. Here are suggestions to help keep costs down.

- Avoid using photos or shaded illustrations; use line art instead.

- Stick with standard paper sizes.

- Avoid using bleeds (ink that goes to the edge of the paper).

- Avoid reverses (large areas requiring heavy ink coverage) as they are harder to print.

- See if your quick printer has color days when a color costs little or nothing extra. (My printer does reflex blue business cards on Tuesdays.)

- Use black ink on a white, brilliant, or deep shade of paper instead of using two color inks.

- Use a brilliant or deep-colored ink on colored paper instead of using two color inks.

- Use one brilliant ink color instead of using two common ink colors.

- Use an attractive paper and one ink color instead of using two ink colors.

- Use your printer's house stock.

- Do your checks carefully. The earlier in the printing process a change is made, the less expensive it is.

- Give yourself as much time as possible to avoid last-minute rush charges.

- Ask the printer for ways to save money on your particular job.

### Be prepared for mistakes

Mistakes happen during the printing process. There are several steps to the printing process of any publication, sales literature, or business forms. Things can and do regularly go wrong. Here are some of the many things that could happen.

- Something slips past you on the blueline proofs.
- The paper doesn't arrive at the print shop on time.
- The ink takes longer to dry than expected.
- A person important to the printing process becomes ill.
- There are bindery or folding problems.
- The black ink isn't black enough.
- The colors are wrong.
- The color turns out darker than you expected.
- The color turns out lighter than you expected.
- The color looks awful on the paper.
- Solid areas of ink are streaky.
- The piece comes out crooked.
- Your job is printed on the wrong paper.
- The printed piece wasn't scored (creased), so it cracks at the fold.
- Something is left out.
- You don't ask how much a change will cost before it is made.
- The project wasn't drilled so it can be put into a binder.
- The project was delivered to the wrong place.
- You assumed something you should not have.

Try to anticipate problems before they arise.

### Evaluate the print job

After the printing has been completed, evaluate the quality of the job to determine if you'll work with this printer in the future.

- Was the ink color right?
- Was the paper color right?
- Was there overprinting or underprinting?
- Are there smudges on the finished job?

- Was the ink consistently applied across the page, or were there lighter colored areas?
- How does the finishing of the project look?
- Were any holes that needed to be drilled into the paper drilled, and was this done cleanly?
- Did the printer deliver on the date promised?
- Does the invoice agree with the quotation from the printer?

Service bureaus provide a link between computers and commercial print shops.

## Dealing with Service Bureaus

Eventually, all of us will have to deal with a service bureau for better quality output or color proofs. Service bureaus, often called service providers, provide a link between computers and commercial print shops. Some print shops have imagesetting facilities and can output the film for you. Other print shops will take your diskette and farm it out to a service bureau.

### Higher resolution output

Most desktop publishers have a laser printer with 300 or 600 dots per inch (dpi), which is fine for proofreading your projects and producing business forms. But if you want better quality, use a service bureau, which has imagesetting equipment capable of outputting paper or film at 1,270, 2,250, 3,350 dpi, or better. The type will appear crisper, and screens and photos will have a finer line screen. Also, your pages can be output directly to film so your print shop doesn't have to do it, and you save money!

### Color proofs

Most service bureaus have color printers so your documents can be output in color and checked.

After your film has been made, you can have blueline proofs, color overlay proofs, or color laminated proofs made from the film. Many commercial printers will not start a process color job without a color proof made from the film.

### Disk conversion

If someone supplies you with a diskette of material produced on another computer platform, your computer may not be able to read the diskette. For example, artwork created on a Macintosh computer for your publication created on a Windows computer can be converted so it can be "read" by other computers. If you don't have a conversion software program, a service bureau can transfer the information onto a diskette formatted for your computer. See Chapter 8 for guidelines on how to convert files from one computer platform to another.

### Scans

Service bureaus can scan (digitally capture) your photographs and illustrations for use in your computer-generated layout. Remember, color images require a lot of memory and may not fit onto a 1.4 megabyte diskette. The information must be saved on an external storage device such as a CD-ROM or removable media drive.

### Slides

Some service bureaus can produce slides or transparencies from your computer-generated artwork. Slide presentation programs such as Adobe Persuasion can be output on 35mm slides.

### Archiving onto Photo CD

Most service bureaus can take your removable media drive cartridges and save the information onto a CD-ROM for you. You can then re-use the cartridge. A CD-ROM provides almost permanent storage for your electronic files. You will be able to read the files from your CD, but you will not be able to save changes to them unless you have your own writable CD recorder. A photo CD can hold about 650 megabytes of electronic information or about 100 color photographs.

### Supplying original graphic files

When importing a graphic into a page layout program such as Adobe PageMaker, a dialog box appears which explains the amount of memory the graphic will occupy, for example, 358K. If you click on the Yes button, the photo is anchored with the document and increases the file size of the document by that amount. If you click on the No button, a preview of the graphic is saved with the document, but you will need the original graphic file to output it.

If you produce a four-page newsletter in PageMaker and click the Yes button to every photo, you probably won't be able to save this document on a diskette. The document — with every photo embedded — would be too large to save on a diskette.

## Checklist 4
## Service Bureau Checklist

☐ Check each page and reference number carefully.

☐ Are you providing a QuarkXPress or PageMaker document? Most service bureaus output from QuarkXPress, so if you have a Photoshop or Illustrator file, check to see if you should import it into QuarkXPress or Adobe PageMaker.

☐ Did you include all the original scans and illustrations? Some page layout programs save a low-resolution preview of the picture with the file, but the service bureau needs the original images to output the document properly.

☐ Did you change the name of any of your scanned artwork or illustrations after importing them into QuarkXPress or PageMaker? Remember, Quark knows what the artwork is called and where it was saved, so don't change it after importing it.

☐ Does your service bureau have the fonts to output your file correctly? You may have used Adobe Garamond and your service bureau may use ITC Garamond. If it outputs the file with different fonts, the text may re-flow.

☐ In QuarkXPress, you can choose Font Usage to see a list of the fonts used in your document. To supply fonts to a service bureau for outputting, copy the font from the Fonts folder in your System folder to your diskette.

☐ Did you supply a laser output with the file so the service bureau knows how it should look?

☐ Did you properly label the diskette or tape so the service bureau knows who it belongs to and the name of the client or job to be output?

☐ Did you supply all the necessary information on how to output your file? Most service bureaus provide a form to fill in: paper or film? line screen on photos? what size of paper or film? how soon do you want the job? etc.

☐ Did you delete all blank pages from the back of the document? If your service bureau outputs them, it will charge you.

☐ Are your photos grayscale, process color, or duotone? RGB (red, green, blue) colors are not used in the printing industry, so avoid them.

Supply a laser proof with your computer file.

QuarkXPress handles imported images differently. It saves a preview of the picture with the file, but maintains a link to the original photo. When you save a four-page newsletter in QuarkXPress, you're saving a preview of the picture with the document and maintaining a link to the original photo. Quark documents are almost always smaller than those created in PageMaker.

Quark knows what you named the original photo and where you saved it, so don't re-name it or move it! If you send your file to a service bureau for output, don't forget to send the graphic files as well.

## Supplying computer files

Here are some suggestions for preparing your computer files for the service bureau or commercial print shop with imagesetting facilities:

(a) Supply a laser proof with your computer file. It can be a reduced version or a proofread copy. If you're preparing a color job, do color separations so that both you and your service bureau know that the project will separate properly. If you're sending your file via modem, fax a proof as well.

(b) Delete empty pages if you don't want them to be printed. Sometimes, when you import a story, the text will create additional pages. If you reduce the type size on the first page, the text may fit onto one page, so the second page is now blank. Delete it. Some service bureaus include a page range on their order form.

(c) Avoid renaming printer fonts. You can rename your screen fonts, but the printer fonts can be found only if the printer font names have not been modified.

(d) You can't make changes to a PostScript file. After creating a document, you could choose Destination: File in the print dialog box. This creates a PostScript file or "print to disk." By creating a PostScript file, you don't need fonts or graphics used in your document. PostScript files cannot be converted back to QuarkXPress files, which means that a service bureau cannot make any changes.

(e) Avoid using TrueType fonts in color documents. If you choose to use them, don't ask your service bureau to trap them or convert them to curves.

(f) If you save a QuarkXPress page as an EPS (Encapsulated PostScript), you cannot make changes to it unless you have the original QuarkXPress document.

(g) If you're not sure about trapping, don't try to adjust the trapping specifications in your QuarkXPress documents. Have your service bureau apply trapping electronically or pay someone to manually trap the file.

(h) QuarkXPress cannot trap imported graphics. You must trap files in the program you used to create them.

(i) Create simple documents. Every text box you draw, every graphic you import (even if it's the same one over and over), every time you change a font, every time you use 14 spaces (instead of a single tab), and each time you use four returns (instead of a space before or a space after) to add space between paragraphs, you increase the complexity, the size, and the chance of a problem.

(j) Take responsibility for your job. Proofread it carefully before you send it to a service bureau.

(k) Your electronic files are yours, but if the service bureau creates additional files, those files belong to them.

Before taking a file to a service bureau or print shop with imagesetting facilities, it is important to check to make sure you've included everything. Checklist 4 will help you save time and money. When it comes to getting your documents printed correctly, good communication with the service bureau is vital.

## Dealing with Contractors

You may need to hire a writer, editor, or proofreader depending on the project and on what services the client expects your desktop publishing business to provide. You may also want to hire one of these professionals to help you with creating promotional material for your business.

### Assigning projects

When dealing with other suppliers, it is important that they know what you expect from them and how you plan to pay them. Misunderstandings can ruin a good friendship or a business relationship. If you have to assign a project to someone else, here is a list of things that should be discussed with the writer, editor, photographer, illustrator, or desktop publisher:

Someone other than the writer should edit your publications and sales literature.

- The purpose of the piece.
- The approximate length of the piece.
- The nature of the target audience.
- Sources of background material.
- The timeline for the piece.
- When the first draft is due.
- Who else is working on the piece.
- How the piece is to be submitted (on paper, on disk, negatives, slides, number of copies).
- How much time you expect the contractor will put into it.
- The amount and schedule of payments.

## Hiring a writer

Although many clients supply copy for publications and promotional materials for you to layout, some clients may want you to coordinate the entire project, including writing the copy. If you have writing skills, you could write and edit the copy yourself, or you could sub-contract the work out to a writer.

You can pay a writer an hourly rate, by article or column, or a negotiated per-project fee. The average rate for a writer is $200 to $400 per page for a two- to four-page newsletter; the four- to eight-page rate is $500 to $1,000. The per hour rate varies from $20 to $60. Rates may vary depending on geographic location and the state of the economy.

A standard 8 ½" x 11" newsletter has approximately 800 words of body text per page. This will vary depending on your page design and the typeface you are using. If you want two articles per page, then you could pay the writer to write a 400-word article at an established rate.

Avoid signing any long-term contracts with the writer until you feel comfortable with the writer's work and your ability to judge the quality of the writing.

## Hiring an editor

If you are coordinating a project, you may need to sub-contract work out to an editor. After your document has been written, it should be edited for spelling and grammatical errors, sentence structure, clarity of expression, consistency, and organization.

Someone other than the writer should edit your publications and sales literature. If your budget does not allow for hiring an editor, ask a friend or associate to perform this function. If you hired a writer, perhaps you can act as the editor.

The hourly rate for an editor is $12 to $50. Some editors are paid a flat rate of $15 per page. Rates vary depending on your locale and the experience and qualifications of the editor.

Make sure your editor reviews past issues and projects and understands your philosophy, content, mission statement, and target market.

### Hiring a proofreader

A proofreader reads final copy, or proof, to detect errors. A family member or a friend may have the skills and interest in this position, or you can advertise for a part-time proofreader. Proofreaders charge $10 to $40 per hour. Choose someone who can work within your time frame. It is best not to have the writer or editor proofread the work. Since the writer and editor are involved in content, style, and flow of information, they may let minor mistakes slip by. The desktop publisher or typesetter who typeset the publication should not proofread the project either, for the same reasons.

Be sure to discuss duties and deadlines with the proofreader.

### Hiring a designer

You may wish to hire a designer to design a publication or sales piece with guidelines for point size, typeface, grids, and overall page design. When hiring a designer, be specific about how you want the design presented. It could be supplied as templates with style sheets in the computer program of your choice, or it may be presented as hard copy only. It could also be presented as a marker rendering. What are you expecting the designer to create: page and type design, nameplate, standing heads, or logos? Be specific.

Most designers charge by the hour or by the project. Make sure you get a written estimate and establish a deadline for completion of the required design elements. Hourly design fees range from $20 to $100 per hour, depending on the reputation of the designer and how much creativity is required. Outside supplies and materials are usually extra charges. Designers usually mark up outside supplies such as printing by 10 percent to 35 percent.

A designer can also be used on an ongoing basis to layout your projects.

### Hiring a desktop publisher

There are times when you may need to hire another desktop publisher to complete a project for you. For example, if you don't think you'll meet a deadline, you might hire someone to help you. Or perhaps you need another desktop publisher to perform a specialized task that you don't feel qualified to produce. For example, you may require the assistance of an expert when doing your first process color job, or if a client wants you to put his or her publication on-line or onto a CD-ROM and you're not sure how to do it. If you get really busy, you might consider hiring a desktop publisher to work with you on a regular basis.

Some desktop publishers are creative and can design attractive publications, efficient business forms, or appealing brochures. Others stick to the typesetting and layout of a publication on a regular basis. When hiring a desktop publisher, ask to see samples of recent work. Producing color on a desktop computer is not easy and is often performed incorrectly. Make sure the desktop publisher isn't taking on more than he or she is capable of.

Does the desktop publisher know about trapping and overprinting? An art director I know spent $13,000 at a service bureau because he hired a desktop publisher to produce a color brochure with several logos. The brochure looked beautiful on the computer monitor, but the desktop publisher didn't understand trapping and color separations, so the service bureau had to do it. If four-color work is expected, make sure you're supplied with camera-ready artwork which has trapping and color separations.

Most desktop publishers charge an hourly rate of $25 to $125. Desktop publishing has become very competitive. Moonlighters may give away their desktop publishing service for $15 to $20 per hour. But, if you plan to desktop publish full time for more than a year, you will likely need to charge $45 or more per hour to meet expenses. Highly skilled desktop publishers who provide specialized services such as multimedia presentations, CD-ROM authoring, Web page design, or process color publications can demand more money per hour.

Outside supplies and materials are extra. Like designers, desktop publishers mark up outside expenses by 10 percent to 35 percent.

Do you want a diskette supplied? Do you want laser printouts or imagesetting on paper or film? If you're supplied with negative film for four-color work, do you require overlay proofs or laminated proofs? Ask your printer or the desktop publisher.

### Hiring a photographer

Like other creative services, you must be specific when dealing with photographers. What do you want them to supply?

A photographer may charge a location fee for traveling to the photo shoot. Some professional photographers will not supply negative film, but will probably give you a contact sheet made from the negatives that shows all the photos. Pick out the ones you want produced and the photographer will charge for each print for one-time use only. Rates will vary depending on whether the photos are color or black and white, the size of the print, the experience of the photographer, and the type of assignment.

Location fees could be a flat rate and an additional hourly rate for the photographer's time. My photographer charges a flat location fee of $75, plus an hourly rate of $25 for labor, plus $50 for each 5" x 7" black-and-white photograph. All photographs are for one-time use only. I've had other photographers who supplied the roll of film and I took it to an imaging lab to have scanned onto a Kodak Photo CD. It's important to discuss your needs with a photographer before starting.

### Working with writers and contributors

As discussed earlier, many desktop publishers coordinate an entire project. This may include hiring writers, editors, proofreaders, photographers, and printers. After establishing what needs to be written, you can look for contributing writers, including freelancers.

Contributors provide new perspectives, new voices, and fresh air to a publication. A freelancer or unpaid contributor can make personal comments and take stands on issues that are inappropriate for the editor of a publication, who must try to reflect the views of all readers.

I once produced a newsletter for an interior decorator which was distributed free to homes in an affluent area of the city. The front page always had an interview with a satisfied client including before and after photographs. It would have been difficult for the

A writer should know before starting an assignment how many words you expect.

owner of the business to write unbiased articles or to solicit honest comments from past clients. So I hired a professional journalist with excellent interview techniques and good writing skills to do so.

Establish guidelines before you assign any stories. It is important that the writer and the editor have a clear understanding of what is expected.

The first step in drafting guidelines is, once again, to know your audience. Make sure the writer understands the tone you want to take. Is it technical, personal, promotional, or a news item?

Second, how long should the article be? A writer should know before starting the assignment how many words you expect. For example, an 8 ½" x 11" newsletter can fit about 800 words on each page, depending on the typeface, type size, and graphics. You don't want the writer to submit five times more copy than you can publish — that only creates more work for you.

What format do you want — promotional copy or editorial? Do you want a checklist, opinion piece, or detailed investigative report?

Your guidelines should specify whether you expect the writer to supply photographs, charts, drawings, or other graphics. They should also state what you will pay, if you are using professional freelance writers. When using contributors who are experts in their field rather than professional writers who depend on freelance fees for their living, you may consider paying an honorarium of $100 to $200. For in-house experts, how about rewarding them with a certificate of appreciation or letter from the president?

And don't forget the most important guideline of all: the deadline.

When you hire a writer, go over the guidelines with the writer, and ask for questions. Add to the guidelines if necessary.

## CHAPTER 12

# OPPORTUNITIES WITH THE INTERNET

*As the game changes, so must the players.*

— BARBARA A. FANSON

Internet fever, or "the Gold Rush of the 1990s," has made the biggest and fastest change in the computer industry. The Internet's World Wide Web is an increasingly popular medium for distributing and viewing information in the form of pages of text and graphics. Desktop publishers should have access to the Internet for four important reasons. First, you can use the Internet to find solutions for computer or software problems and download software updates and patches, as well as to purchase software such as fonts, clip art, and stock photography. Second, the Internet can be used to promote your business. Third, the Internet can be used to access information if you are also creating content for the publication you are working on. And finally, there are financial opportunities for desktop publishers who can design Web pages for their clients.

## What is a Web Site?

A Web site is a group of related pages that reside together on a Web server. A home page is the introductory page to your Web site, and the default page on which your Web site will open when someone visits.

## An Opportunity to Promote Your Business

You can use the Internet to post information and promotions about your own business or services. Here are some points to consider:

- Why are you setting up a Web site? Are you setting up a site to sell products or services?

- Are you trying to market your capabilities by building awareness?

- Who is the site for: current customers or potential customers?

- What is your approach to customer service?

- How will you attract surfers to your site?

- How will you encourage repeat business or more visits to the site?

- Do you wish to become a resource for information?

- Can you use hits on the site to build a data base of potential clients?

- Are there other directories or related topics you could tie into your site?

- What will you include in your site?

- How can you keep your site fast to download?

- How often will you change the copy in your site?

## Creating Web Pages

### Hypertext Markup Language (HTML)

Every page on the Web is described using the Hypertext Markup Language (HTML). Some software programs require you to learn the actual HTML codes to format the text and graphics on a page while other programs automatically code.

## Layout considerations

HTML is a set of tags for a sequence of text and graphics, with hypertext links. It was not designed as a full page-description language. An HTML page is one column of continuous text with graphics that flow along with the text, as if they were characters themselves.

Web pages can contain links to other Web pages.

You cannot control the size of the page and the width of the text column, because the page proportions and line breaks vary depending on the size of the monitor or window in which the page is viewed, and the size of the font the reader chooses in a Web browser. As a guideline, you might design for the line length produced by a Web browser using a default font on a 640 x 480-pixel screen.

Because graphics are part of the text stream in HTML, you cannot specify a precise horizontal and vertical position for a graphic. If you position a graphic at the bottom right of a page as it appears on your monitor and a reader decides to make the window narrower, the graphic will probably move to the next line down and may end up on the left side of the page.

## Typographical considerations

Many type specifications cannot be controlled on a Web page; line breaks, letter spacing, and word spacing, for example, are determined by the size of the window and the font settings in a Web browser. The following type characteristics are controlled by Web browsers and cannot be specified in most Web page design applications:

- Font, type size, and leading
- Font width (horizontal scale)
- Tracking/kerning
- Strikethrough, outline, shadow, reverse, superscript, and subscript type styles
- Tab positions
- Spacing before or after a paragraph

## Web links

Links are one of the most significant differences between printed pages and Web pages. Web pages can contain hypertext links to other Web pages or to other parts of the same page. When you click on a link, the Web browser takes you to the page set as a destination for the link. Links appear as specially marked text or images on the page.

Links allow you to create nonsequential arrangements of pages in your Web site. Instead of having one page follow another, as in a book, several links may be sprinkled throughout each page, with each link leading directly to another page containing links to even more pages. You can link pages into the most appropriate structure for the information you are conveying.

## Setting up a Web Site

Most Internet Service Providers provide space for personal Web sites; these are usually included in the basic cost of the account. These sites are fine for presenting and promoting your services and Web design skills. Business accounts that provide more space and functionalism can cost on average $75 to $200.

### Lay out the Web pages

Before you begin creating Web pages, you should have an idea of how your pages will look and how they will link together.

Create a rough sketch for each page, setting up areas for text and images. Decide where you will place links and what elements you'll provide for navigating among pages.

Sketch the entire site, showing the relationships between the pages and how they link to each other and to pages outside your site. Develop a logical structure for the names of the files making up your site.

### Design your Web site

Who will design your Web site? If you have a Web page design software program and the necessary knowledge, you can design your own Web page. With some software programs, you don't need to know Hypertext Markup Language (HTML). Or, hire someone who specializes in Web page design.

You can prepare a site on a computer away from the Web server and then upload, or send a copy of the site to the Web server, where it will be published electronically to the world.

Here are some tips to help you design an effective Web site. Remember, if your site is not worth the download time, that is, if it is not attractive, interesting, or informative, surfers will not return.

- The first screen cover page should have a table of contents or summary.

- Use buttons to take a viewer to the respective section of the site.

- Use eye-catching graphics to entice readers to stay at your site.

- Image maps are effective methods of promoting other sections of your site. When viewers move their mouse over a "hot spot" or programmed area of a graphic, the mouse pointer or cursor will change into a finger to indicate a hot spot. When the mouse is clicked on the hot spot, the cursor will jump to another spot or another page in the site.

- Include links for the viewer to other sites directly related to topics in your Web site.

- Links throughout the copy can move viewers to other areas of your site or to other Web sites.

- Small graphics can be effective. Be sure to keep them small to increase access speeds.

- Web graphics should be designed for monitors with 72 ppi (pixels per inch) resolutions; scan photographs with a low resolution of 72 ppi.

- Video or QuickTime clips are great for viewers who have a computer equipped with the necessary software.

Publicize your Web site on any promotions and business stationery you have.

## Maintain Your Web Site

Most Web sites require periodic maintenance. For example, you may need to restructure your site as it grows, make corrections to information on the pages, or add, delete, or rename files. You can make the changes in a Web page design program, but remember, deleting, moving, or renaming files can break your links.

## Promote Your Web Site

There is no use setting up a Web site if no one visits it. Publicize your site on any promotions and business stationery you have.

Promote your Web site in a print publication, if you have one. Advertise in local computer papers, Internet publications, or local newspapers. Register your site with a variety of search engines so that people searching on the Net for your type of services will find your site.

## Designing Web Pages For Clients

Since you already have, or are planning to buy, the equipment necessary for desktop publishing and print production, why not turn your pages into "Net profits?" Why not discuss with the client the possibility of putting one of your client's print publications on-line? You already have the client; just add another service and make more money from the same client with your ability to create a presence for him or her on the Net.

If you put the publication on the Internet, keep these tips in mind:

- Make sure readers can find the publication on the Net.
- Attract viewers to the site; include a good feature article.
- Be consistent and update the content regularly.
- Don't try to recreate the content of a print publication, or viewers will have no reason to buy the print publication.
- Deal with the same topics as in the print publication, but from different angles.
- Use the Web site to promote articles in future issues of the print publication.
- Publicize the print publication on the Web site and publicize the Web site in the publication.
- Material must be well organized, tight, concise, and broken up into tangible pieces. Use lots of subheads so viewers can scan.

Avoid tables, charts, and graphics that may not work well on-line.

## Helping Clients Who Want to Create Their Own Web Sites

Since design software has made designing a Web site easier to do and more affordable, many businesses choose to produce their own site. So, how do you get clients to hire you if they want to create their own Web sites?

There are two ways you could still get freelance work from a business that wants to design its own Web site. Firstly, you could design the initial Web site and the client could maintain and update it. Or, you could specialize in the more challenging elements of a Web page such as animation, interactive buttons, online forms, database searches, or programming dynamic Web pages. Consider promoting yourself as an expert who can take a Web site from the ordinary to the "extra-ordinary"!

## Pricing Web Page Design

It is difficult to know how to price a Web site you are designing when you begin. What some designers do is establish an hourly rate and then determine how long it will take to design the site. Other designers charge a package price, which includes a predetermined number of pages, photos, artwork, animation, and interactivity.

You could create a fee schedule for various elements of the Web site. For example, you may charge $100 for each animation, interactive button, or page on the site. You could also charge a set price for each page and hope they balance out. Some pages will have more graphics, while others will not have any graphics at all.

To get an idea of what you should charge, check out other designers' Web sites and see what they are doing regarding their fee structures.

## CHAPTER 13

# THE FUTURE OF DESKTOP PUBLISHING

*We have to know what opportunities are going to flourish in the future and make sure we are prepared to meet those needs.*

— JENNY COCO

In the past few years, computers and the desktop publishing industry have changed rapidly. It is hard to predict what it will look like ten or even five years from now. I believe that desktop publishing opportunities will exist in advertising agencies and commercial print shops for many years to come. Though the way we input information and output electronic files may change, a computer will still be used in the process.

## Competing with People from Different Industries

Computers and software programs have come down in price so that more people can afford to purchase them for home or business. In 1988, I was given a quotation of $25,000 to purchase a computer, laser printer, professional software, and cables. Today, I can purchase the same equipment and software for about $6,000.

Unfortunately, as software becomes easier to use and computers are more affordable, there is a noticeable decrease in the quality of literature and presentations. Typesetting, design, and print production courses are often ignored, so we are surrounded by unprofessional examples of computer-generated "artwork."

People who are serious about desktop publishing as a career should learn how to measure type and typeset professionally. They should also learn design and layout basics, as well as prepress and production techniques, and develop an understanding of the printing industry.

Desktop publishing is attracting people from the traditional graphic arts industry and related industries such as journalism, photography, and video production, as well as unrelated fields. Some people are learning desktop publishing so they can offer more services to clients, while others are taking classes to keep their jobs.

Years ago, company newsletter editors would write stories and farm out the production to a typesetting house. Today, writers and editors can purchase affordable computers with easy-to-use software and output print-quality artwork themselves.

Writers and marketing specialists are using computers to prepare publications and promotional material. Photographers are using image-editing software to re-touch photos. Video production experts are turning to computers for video editing or creating electronic presentations.

Since graphic artists will be competing with people from unrelated fields for desktop publishing work, it is important that you specialize in something that you don't think the average person can do. For example, a newsletter editor can learn a page layout program, but how many of them can do a process color publication?

## Changing with the Industry

If you want a profitable desktop publishing business, you must stay abreast of changes in the industry. Purchase computer magazines so you know how the equipment and software are changing and how it effects your business. Do you need to take courses to learn a software program, computer programming, multimedia, Web page design, or print production?

Here are just a few of the changes in the computer and graphic arts industries.

If you want a profitable desktop publishing business, you must stay abreast of changes in the industry.

### Changes in the printing industry

Large commercial print shops have invested in computers and imagesetting equipment so they can produce artwork, archive files, and be able to make changes later. They can also output client-supplied files onto film, paper, plate, or directly to the press. Direct-to-plate technology skips the traditional film stage to produce a plate for the printing press directly from the computer. Direct-to-press technology has computers hooked up to printing presses and skips the film and platemaking stage.

### Short-run color

Short-run color technology allows a desktop publisher to output a file from a computer directly to a color press without the use of film, stripping, trapping, and platemaking. And short-run color is more affordable for small quantities. I recently had 300 flyers printed from a computer onto an Indigo short-run color press for $350; the quote for traditional printing was $695.

### Faster modems

People now want faster modems to download from the Internet through a telephone line to their computer. When I bought a 9,600 baud modem in 1990 for $750, I was one of the first of my friends to get a modem. By 2003, I was on my fifth modem. I went from a 9,600 to a 14,400 to a 28,500 baud modem to a high-speed telephone line to cable high-speed Internet access.

I purchased the first modem so I could send computer files to my service bureau via the telephone line so it could output the file onto film. Then came the fax modem so I could send computer files directly to someone's fax machine. And then I had to purchase a faster modem to use with the Internet. Eventually I switched again when high-speed access became available.

To be successful, you may have to expand your services to include multimedia, Web page design, electronic presentations, video editing or large format poster printing. You may also specialize in high-end, more advanced design that the average person cannot do, such as four-color work, bigger documents or more pages. Make yourself indispensable by creating outstanding visual elements like photos with special effects, exciting graphs and tables, and interesting page layouts.

Be on the lookout for opportunities; they often come disguised as hard work.

# Barbara Fanson's 24 hot design trends for the future

1. The newsletter industry will continue to grow because of two reasons: businesses have realized that newsletters are an effective method of promotion and desktop publishing makes it faster and easier to produce a newsletter.

2. Unbalanced or irregular columns will be seen more often. Traditionally, columns would align at the bottom.

3. More scholar's margin grid layouts — either one narrow and one wide column or two wide columns and one narrow column.

4. More text wraps with text wrapping around photos or art.

5. Drop shadows on photos add dimension to photos.

6. More feathered edges on photos so they fade out.

7. More publications have photos without a frame.

8. Close cropping photos to remove the background.

9. Collage of two or more photos so one fades into another.

10. Special effects with image-editing software programs.

11. Special filters to alter the image so it looks like an illustration of painting.

12. More rough edges on photos so they resemble a paintbrush swash.

13. Increased use of Photo CDs so photos can be stored on a compact disc.

14. Digital photography will become more popular as the technology improves. With a digital camera, you will not have to purchase film, process film, or scan the image into a computer. In 29 seconds, you will have an image on the computer screen.

15. Increased feathering — altering the leading of one column slightly so it is the same length as the next column.

16. Tighter tracking/kerning so there is less space between characters.

17. Altering the horizontal scale (width of a character) to make the type wider and narrower.

18. More designers will use less traditional typefaces since they have a better selection.

19. More distorting or altering type to create logos or heads.

20. More type on a curve since many desktop publishers have a drawing program.

21. Type in a circle will be very popular as a special logo.

22. Drop shadows on type are popular since many have discovered how to produce a good drop shadow in a photo-editing or graphics program.

23. Increased use of clip art since it can be purchased at a reasonable price.

24. Desktop publishers will evolve into Web page design.